PROFESSIONAL WRESTLING

Other books in the At Issue series:

PROFESSIONAL WRESTLING

Louise I. Gerdes, *Book Editor*

Daniel Leone, *President*
Bonnie Szumski, *Publisher*
Scott Barbour, *Managing Editor*

GREENHAVEN PRESS
SAN DIEGO, CALIFORNIA

THOMSON
™
GALE

Detroit • New York • San Diego • San Francisco
Boston • New Haven, Conn. • Waterville, Maine
London • Munich

Library of Congress Cataloging-in-Publication Data

Professional wrestling / Louise I. Gerdes, book editor.
    p. cm. — (At issue)
    Includes bibliographical references and index.
    ISBN 0-7377-0814-X (pbk. : alk. paper) —
ISBN 0-7377-0815-8 (lib. bdg. : alk. paper)
    1. Wrestling. 2. Wrestling—Social aspects. I. Gerdes, Louise I.
II. At issue (San Diego, Calif.)

GV1195 .P76   2002
796.812—dc21   2001054754

Contents

Introduction

. It is 9 P.M. Monday night, and an announcer asks thousands of professional wrestling fans crowded into a local stadium, "Are you ready to rumble?" A television camera pans the audience as screaming fans of all ages leap to their feet, waving signs and sporting T-shirts that honor their favorite pro wrestling stars. Rock and roll music blares while fireworks explode on either side of a wide ramp that leads to a wrestling ring in the center of the stadium. Stone Cold Steve Austin, with shaved head, bulging muscles, and form-fitting latex wrestling shorts, emerges from backstage to stand defiantly before the crowd, scowling. With a microphone in hand, Austin reveals his elaborate plans to defeat his current nemesis and in the process curses, guzzles beer, parodies biblical verses, and pledges allegiance to no one but himself. Of the more than 7 million people watching at home, some laugh at Austin's bravado, but others, some young children, cheer the man who challenges authority and defies his employer—perhaps secretly wishing that they too could stand up to their boss or the school bully.

What in the 1950s was considered "low brow" entertainment, appealing to a relatively small group of people, has since become big business. Pro wrestling is the most popular programming on cable television—more popular than news, sports, drama, comedy, home shopping, cartoons, and soap operas. The World Wrestling Federation (WWF), developed by controversial wrestling promoter Vince McMahon, has several top-rated cable television wrestling programs seen by more than 7 million viewers each week. On March 23, 2001, the WWF purchased its rival organization, World Championship Wrestling (WCW), now maintaining what some claim is a virtual monopoly over pro wrestling programming. WWF home video sales routinely rank first in sports video, and its action figures outsold Pokemon in 1999. WWF websites consistently rank in the top ten when counted among established sport sites such as ESPN.com, and they are the first nonpornographic sites to turn streaming video into profits. The stock market values the family-owned WWF at more than $1 billion.

The current popularity of pro wrestling is largely the fruit of McMahon's labors. During the 1980s McMahon began to consolidate the country's regional wrestling organizations, which were relatively small and obscure, into a national federation, the WWF. He also began to incorporate elements of popular culture, such as rock and roll music and special effects, into wrestling programs. McMahon officially proclaimed what fans had known for years, wrestling was not "real," but "sports entertainment." He developed complex behind-the-scenes sagas that combined action-adventure with soap opera story lines filled with sex and intrigue. The story lines star his own family as well as the larger-than-life wrestlers themselves.

In 1988 media mogul Ted Turner created the WCW and began to

compete with McMahon's WWF. Some argue this competition created a "top this" philosophy in pro wrestling programming that contributed to its increasingly outrageous and controversial content. Between 1996 and 1998, while the WWF was embroiled in a steroid scandal and allegations of sexual misconduct, the WCW overcame the WWF in the ratings. After being acquitted of steroid abuse, however, McMahon and the WWF came back with a vengeance. McMahon hired writers from *The Conan O'Brien Show* and MTV, who were in touch with wrestling's target audience—young adult males—and WWF matches further tested the bounds of civility while the audience for pro wrestling continued to grow.

Although pro wrestling programming provides entertainment for millions of fans, tragically, when some young people have imitated the antics of pro wrestlers, the consequences have been lethal. On July 28, 1999, in Fort Lauderdale, Florida, twelve-year-old Lionel Tate killed his six-year-old playmate Tiffany Eunick. The 180-pound Tate told police that he grabbed Eunick in a bear hug, then dropped her, causing her to hit her head on a table. He later told police that he swung her around and her head struck a cast-iron railing. The medical examiner said that the injuries of forty-eight-pound Eunick included a fractured skull, a lacerated liver, a broken rib, internal hemorrhaging, and more than thirty other bruises and breaks. Prosecutors sought a first-degree murder conviction for Tate. "This was a continued beating with fists and feet," said prosecutor Ken Padowitz. "Lionel Tate used his body as a weapon."

Tate's attorneys, however, argued that their client was innocent of murder, maintaining that Eunick's death was a tragic accident. Tate was influenced by the theatrics of pro wrestling, they claimed, and was imitating the stunts executed by WWF star Dwayne Johnson, whose pro wrestling stage name is "The Rock." To support their defense, Tate's attorneys subpoenaed The Rock and other pro wrestlers to testify about how they make their televised action appear authentic. The judge, however, limited the testimony to Tate's love of wrestling, and on January 25, 2001, Tate was convicted of first-degree murder. On March 9, 2001, then fourteen, Tate was sentenced to life in prison without parole. At the sentencing hearing, Tate's mother, Kathleen Grossett-Tate, testified that her son was not aware that he faced life in prison for his actions. "How do you tell a child you're going to prison for the rest of your life for playing?"

The death of Tiffany Eunick was not an isolated incident. In Hudson County, Georgia, a four-year-old child jumped up and down on a fifteen-month-old baby and killed him after their babysitter left to buy cigarettes. The babysitter had put on a WWF video to entertain the children while he was gone. According to the prosecutor, the four-year-old was mimicking what he saw on the pro wrestling video and thought he could do so without permanently harming the baby. On January 16, 1999, in Yakima, Washington, twelve-year-old Jason Whala, an avid pro wrestling fan, killed his nineteen-month-old cousin William Sweet with a "Jackknife Power Bomb" when Sweet would not stop crying. Whala picked Sweet up over his head, turned the child toward him, and slammed him to the ground. Whala was convicted of second-degree felony murder.

Is pro wrestling programming responsible for the tragic deaths of these children? Some authorities do not think that small children can effectively tell the difference between the scripted violence in pro wrestling and the real thing. Sports psychology professor Steve Danish says that children under eight cannot distinguish between reality and fantasy when they watch wrestling violence. "If they watch a movie on HBO they understand more quickly that that isn't real. But this is a 'sport,' and they probably don't see that this isn't real."

What about the deaths that came at the hands of Lionel Tate and Jason Whala, who are teenagers and therefore presumably able to understand the consequences of their dangerous acts? Is pro wrestling to blame? According to Whala's attorney, Adam Moore, "Parents should wake up. This is a wake-up call. Don't let your little boys watch [professional wrestling] or do so at grave risk." Critics argue that teenagers exposed to the violence of pro wrestling week after week become desensitized to violence. Pro wrestlers are glamorous, critics claim, and their violent behaviors are therefore perceived to be acceptable. Moreover, pro wrestling "reaches into [teens'] fantasies about being able to put someone down and have that person be begging or hurt," says Danish. Although Danish does not believe watching pro wrestling will in itself desensitize young people to violence, it may reinforce "what may be happening elsewhere in that child's life," including exposure to violence in the home or at school.

Besides perhaps contributing to random acts of youth violence, the popularity of pro wrestling has also led to the phenomena of backyard wrestling. In backyards across North America, young people, often with the support of parents, have constructed makeshift wrestling rings in which they strike each other with steel chairs, trash cans, guitars, ladders, mattress frames, and two-by-fours, often permanently maiming or killing themselves. Although the WWF officially discourages these backyard leagues and refuses to watch or recruit from homemade wrestling videos, many participants aspire to be "discovered" by the professional leagues. Twenty-one-year-old Luke Hadley of Sturgeon Bay, Wisconsin, has had ten concussions, a broken arm, and a broken tailbone and sports hundreds of scars and a few soft spots in his brain. "Sometimes I want to say stuff, and no words come out," says Hadley, but "in twenty years, after I hit it big, I'll be able to afford all the surgeries I need." Unfortunately for Hadley, backyard wrestlers face near impossible odds as the professional federations generally recruit only professional and collegiate athletes.

Pro wrestling promoters acknowledge that the deaths of these children are tragic and that backyard wrestling is a horrifying, dangerous trend. However, promoters claim they have issued numerous public service announcements warning against the practice of duplicating the pro wrestling stunts seen on television. They agree that pro wrestlers are seen as role models for young children, but they insist that pro wrestlers should be held no more accountable for children's injuries than other professional athletes. Supporters ask why pro wrestlers should be blamed for the injuries caused by those who imitate them when no one blames professional football players when young people are hurt emulating them. According to Mick Foley, a veteran professional wrestler and author, "Calling pro wrestling violent and football family entertainment is an incredible double standard."

Supporters suggest that if parents allow their children to watch wrestling programs, they have the responsibility to explain that the wrestling is fake and to teach their children appropriate values and provide alternatives to violence. Editor Eric E. Jenkins writes, "The job of supervising children who desire to imitate wrestlers falls on the parents or the guardians of these children. As often as professional wrestlers tell the world that what they do is scripted, choreographed, and well rehearsed but they still get injured, someone else has to make sure that the message is received by the children." Pro wrestling, supporters argue, should not be blamed for the unfortunate deaths of unsupervised children who fail to heed the warnings or have these warnings interpreted for them. Jenkins writes, "If a man walks into a bar, utters the words, 'Go ahead, make my day,' and then shoots the bartender, you are not going to hold Clint Eastwood responsible. You also cannot blame wrestling if a child kills another child pretending to be a wrestler."

The debate over the influence of pro wrestling programming is far from over. Some critics claim the content of pro wrestling programming is not only too violent, but also too vulgar and overtly sexual for the children who watch these programs. Others argue that for adults and children alike, pro wrestling encourages a culture of confrontation and disrespect. Those who support pro wrestling counter that the matches are obviously "fake" and less violent than other prime-time programs. Promoters, they claim, are simply providing adult entertainment to meet the demand of millions of fans who enjoy pro wrestling. Parents, they insist, not pro wrestling's self-appointed censors, must determine what programs children watch. These and other perspectives are presented in *At Issue: Professional Wrestling.*

1

The Birth of Modern Professional Wrestling: An Overview

Lynn Rosellini

Lynn Rosellini is a senior writer for U.S. News & World Report. *She writes on controversial issues, including entertainment and sports.*

During the 1980s Vince McMahon consolidated smaller regional wrestling tours into a national company, the World Wrestling Federation (WWF), which evolved into a multimillion-dollar industry that has become part of American culture. The WWF's wrestling shows are filled with violence, obscenity, and simulated sex. McMahon claims, however, that movies contain more sex and violence, and his shows simply reflect the world at large. Although social critics argue wrestling's violence and vulgarity send the wrong message to young people, McMahon claims his job is to entertain—parents have the responsibility of monitoring what their kids watch. While people continue to question the impact of pro wrestling on society, the WWF's programs receive some of the highest ratings on cable TV. Some authorities explain that the WWF's archetypal cast of characters reflect shared emotional experiences that appeal to every type of fan.

The child bolted upright in his bed, awakened by screams, his mother's screams, crackling through the thin walls of the house trailer and shattering the blackness of the North Carolina night. Creeping out of bed, the boy peered into the next room, where his 200-pound stepfather bent over his mother's crouched form, bloodying her face with his fist. "Hey, what are you guys doing?" cried the startled child, and the man spun and grabbed the 6-year-old's hair, bringing a closed fist hard across his face until the cheeks were bloody and the child whimpered and fled. Later, in his bed, the boy would weep.

His stepfather was an electrician, and he used whatever tools were on hand to beat his child: wire, screwdrivers, a pipe wrench. The lesson seemed simple—violence solves problems—and the boy learned it well as he grew, fighting, drinking, and disrupting school so often he was finally expelled. Later, as a young man, when he had tamed his rebelliousness and begun to work for the old-time wrestling promoter who was his real father, he discovered he could draw on his violent past. In time, he would create a world of fury and mayhem so big and so bad that it made his childhood home look like Disneyland. But this time, there would be a difference: This time, the bad guys would work for him.

A controversial captain of industry

"Did you see it, wasn't that cool?" Vince McMahon gasps, out of breath and dripping with beer and perspiration. He has just lurched off the set of a live audience taping of *Smackdown!* in New Haven, Conn., where he was "bashed" with a metal chair and ended the match spread-eagled on the canvas. *Smackdown!* is just one of the hugely successful shows produced by McMahon's World Wrestling Federation (WWF), which in the past 17 years has taken professional wrestling from a marginal, back-alley sport to nothing short of a new American art form: "sports entertainment," he calls it, a bizarre melange of rock music, pyrotechnics, soap opera, and athleticism staged before frenzied crowds. McMahon's Monday night two-hour *Raw Is War*, filled with lewdness, simulated sex, prostitutes, and profanities, is the No. 1-rated show on cable TV, outpacing even *Monday Night Football* among male teens and edging out its slightly less raunchy rival, World Championship Wrestling's (WCW) *Monday Nitro*. The two competing tours produce 15 hours of weekly TV, attracting a whopping 35 million viewers.

> *The man responsible for the wrestling boom is every bit as much a paradox as his product.*

But McMahon has wrought far more than just a popular TV show. With a bevy of spinoffs—two magazines, videos, a Web site, T-shirts, action figures, and even cologne—WWF and its competitor, WCW, have managed to infiltrate the fantasies of an entire generation of young boys. In certain parts of the country, it's hard to find a male teen who can't identify Stone Cold Steve Austin (the beer-swilling, shiny-domed WWF superstar) or Goldberg (the grimacing, shiny-domed WCW superstar). Overseas, professional wrestlers are often the face of American culture: WWF programming is currently beamed to 120 countries and translated into 11 languages.

Yet the extent to which wrestling's violence and vulgarity affect society—and especially young people—is far from clear. Certainly, nobody claims that pile driving one's enemies or ranting obscenities is a testament to cultural progress. McMahon says he is just reflecting the world around him. But a host of social critics—educators, pediatricians, and parents—argue that McMahon is doing far worse, by pitching to a vulnerable young audience the vilest messages of our times: Racial stereotypes are OK. Ogling women and making crude remarks are the marks of a man. It's cool to tell people to "Kiss my a—" or "Suck it." And if you disagree with someone, "bash" them.

Current events only confuse the picture. In the aftermath of the tragic shootings in Littleton, Colo., many Americans are debating whether the United States has a special culture of violence in which the link between social ills and televised brutality like wrestling seems all too obvious. Yet there is surprisingly little scientific research to connect the two. In Littleton, both killer and victim apparently watched wrestling. Matthew Kechter, who was killed, was such a WWF fan that his family requested—and received—a special tribute to the victims, which aired on *Raw* in 1999.

[McMahon] is first and foremost an entertainer, he says, and it's the job of parents—not himself—to monitor what kids watch on TV.

The man responsible for the wrestling boom is every bit as much a paradox as his product. Onstage, he is the mean, scowling schemer, "Mr. McMahon," who will lie, cheat, and crack skulls to get the power and money he craves. Offstage, he seems almost guileless. "My job is to entertain the masses at whatever level they want," he says, sipping his 10th cup of coffee of the day in the slick glass-and-marble headquarters of Titan Sports Inc., WWF's parent company. In person, McMahon is an affectionate, affable man with a shiny brown pompadour and a disarming candor. One minute he volunteers intimate details about his marriage (he cheated repeatedly—"It's not something I'm proud of"). The next, he squeezes the arm of his publicist, saying, "I could be better at patting others on the back, right, pal?" This is Vince, the softie who wept the first time he held his son. Vince, who sends his wrestlers out to meet dying kids for the Make-A-Wish Foundation.

The other face of Vince McMahon

Then there is the ready-to-rumble Vince, the aggressive competitor whom a former WWF wrestler once called "an evil guy" who treats wrestlers like "circus animals." This Vince follows a simple code: You hit him, he hits back. In the mid-'90s, after Ted Turner lured away some of McMahon's stars for his competing WCW tour on the cable channels TBS and TNT, McMahon ratcheted up the level of violence and sexuality in *Raw* to new levels—even while admitting that 15 percent of the audience, or more than 1 million viewers, is 11 years old or younger. By February of 1999, the show's mayhem had risen to such levels that an Indiana University–*Inside Edition* study of 50 episodes reported 1,658 instances of grabbing or pointing to one's crotch, 157 instances of an obscene finger gesture, 128 episodes of simulated sexual activity, and 21 references to urination.

"These shows are extremely inappropriate models for children," says Howard Spivak, chairman of the American Academy of Pediatrics' task force on violence. Kids don't always differentiate fantasy from reality, say Spivak and other critics, who point to 30 years of scientific research linking TV violence with increased fear and aggression in children. Although few researchers have zeroed in on televised wrestling, a 1994 Israeli study of third- through sixth-graders showed that after the WWF started airing in Israel in the early 1990s, violent behavior—in the form of mock wrestling matches that often escalated to fighting and injuries—increased "to a degree never known before." When WWF airtime was cut back, the violence among schoolchildren diminished "sharply."

At the New Haven Coliseum the other night, 10-year-old Jim Sabo, a WWF fan since he was 2, sat with his mother watching *Smackdown!* He was holding a sign he had made himself that read, "Suck It." What he likes best about wrestling, Jim says, is "How they all get hurt." His mother, Laurie, says she's not too concerned about the violence. "He understands it's just an act," she says. "But I'm not happy with the nudity and swearing."

Even some of the WWF's own stars think the show goes too far. "I get a little turned off with some of the sexual overtones," says Stone Cold Steve Austin, who in real life is Steve Williams, the father of two young girls. "I don't dig any of that racism."

Conflicting values

But McMahon accepts no blame. For someone who tries to adhere to a moral code in his private life, he seems strangely disconnected from the moral implications of his public persona. McMahon says he values honesty, respect for others, compassion, and equal treatment for all. He gave up his marital infidelities, he says, when he realized he was "hurting a lot of people." He is proud that he hires only "quality human beings."

But when it comes to wrestling, he refuses to play ethics cop. He is first and foremost an entertainer, he says, and it's the job of parents—not himself—to monitor what kids watch on TV. "*Raw* is TV-14," he says, referring to the content rating. "If parents are concerned about content, they should insist their kids watch the [toned-down version] Saturday and Sunday morning, which is more youth friendly." As for obscene finger gestures, they are "done all over the world." And the frequent WWF appearances of an African-American pimp and his "ho's" (whores)? "We're not concerned about being politically incorrect."

Past episodes of *Raw* have featured mock crucifixions, S&M scenes, wrestlers "mooning" the audience and each other, and a woman sucking suggestively on an Italian sausage. Is there a line beyond which McMahon won't go? "You don't see guns, murder, knives," he says. "We resolve our differences physically, in a wrestling ring. How bad is it compared to a Schwarzenegger or Stallone movie?"

He has a point. Wrestling, with its cartoonish characters and faked body slams and pile drivers, seems less real than Mel Gibson mowing down blood-spurting villains with a pump shotgun. Mick Foley, who plays the deranged WWF character Mankind, says that even children's fairy tales have more blood and gore than the WWF. For instance, in *Snow White*, the evil stepmother requests that Snow White's heart be brought to her in a box (the messenger brings a boar's heart, instead). "If we were to air a story line [like that]," Foley says, "we'd have a media uproar requesting that we be thrown off the air."

McMahon has not asked for anyone's heart in a box—yet—but in an odd way, his success rests on wrestling's ability to tap those troves of human archetypes. Mythologist Joseph Campbell once wrote that humans inevitably re-create ancient myths in each new generation. For all its crudeness, professional wrestling plays to just such familiar fables. In *Raw*, the "sport" occupies just 36 minutes of a two-hour show. The rest is an elaborate, soap-opera-style story line detailing a host of feuds, rivalries, grudges, and byzantine subplots.

A myth maker

Playing out the tales is an oddball cast drawn in part from McMahon's own imagination and embellished by his team of writers and stars. McMahon has never read Homer or Carl Jung, but if wrestling did not pay homage to primordial story lines, it seems unlikely that it would have caught on. The Undertaker, the ultimate archetype of darkness, dresses in black, appears in a cloud of smoke, and continually hauls off victims for Satanic rituals. The 7-foot Kane—a mute, scarred misfit in a scary red mask—is right out of the book of Genesis. Another favorite plot, that of a beautiful woman (McMahon's 22-year-old daughter, Stephanie) abducted by a man, sounds a lot like the *Iliad* or even the Hindu epic *Ramayana*. Then there is the staged rebellion of McMahon's son, Shane, against his father. Oedipus Rex, anyone?

Jungian psychologist Polly Young-Eisendrath says these images are instantly recognizable "because everybody has had the same emotional experience." A fan, Patrick Armstrong, 23, puts it this way: "Every member of the population is represented in the WWF."

And at the center of it all is McMahon, who helped build a multimillion-dollar megabusiness from the small-time shows of the early 1980s. On show night, he darts around nonstop, now poring over the script backstage, now huddling with Steve Austin, now stopping to chat with a reporter about his need to "tweak" the show's story line right up until curtain time. Around him roam the lunatic products of his imagination. A beefy, bare-chested wrestler named Triple H watches while a hairdresser arranges his blond tresses in a ponytail. The Big Show, a 500-pound refrigerator of a man, sprays his vast torso and shoulders with oil. Another star, Al Snow, wanders around carrying a mannequin's severed head. "In psychoanalytic terms," he says solemnly, "I'm projecting a non-verbal cry for help." They all seem to like Vince. He is nice to everybody, they say. "This is a mom-and-pop business," says Nicole Bass, a 6-foot, 2-inch bodybuilder who recently joined the show. "It's really a big family back here."

A troubled past

It's certainly a happier family than the one Vincent Kennedy McMahon left back in Havelock, N.C. His mother married five times, and her boy Vince suffered not only from dyslexia but from attention deficit disorder as well. He was so disruptive in school that the authorities gave him a choice: a state reform school or a military academy. Before long, he had earned the dubious honor of being the first cadet in the history of Fishburne Military School in Waynesboro, Va., to be court-martialed. In fact, the only way McMahon got through what is now called East Carolina University was by attending class for five years, taking summer school every year, and petitioning his professors to raise his grades. "Even today I can't spell," he says.

After stints selling paper cups and adding machines, he went to work in 1971 for his father, who promoted wrestling matches throughout the Northeast. With stars like Gorgeous George, wrestling had been a huge hit in the early days of television, featured on all the networks. But by the late 1960s, it had dropped in appeal. McMahon began buying out the regional promoters who controlled the sport and consolidating the smaller tours into a national company. In the early 1980s, he acknowledged that the outcomes of matches were predetermined, freeing wrestling from state regulations. Ten years later, when a federal investigation of steroid use in the WWF threatened to scuttle the company, Vince beat the charges—while admitting he took steroids himself, when they were still legal.

The guy who grew up in a trailer and put cardboard in his shoes to cover the holes now controls a company with revenues of $500 million a year.

It was during the steroid investigation—and a concurrent scandal involving sexual harassment against a WWF executive (not McMahon)—that Ted Turner made his move. Turner signed several WWF stars, including superstar Hulk Hogan, and positioned his *Monday Nitro* directly opposite *Raw*. The WCW shows topped WWF viewership for more than a year and a half. Irate, McMahon charged Turner with theft of ideas, and his lawsuit—and Turner's countersuit—are pending.

In the end, though, the competition apparently helped them both. Far from mercifully receding, professional wrestling is threatening to expand. Life is good now for McMahon. The guy who grew up in a trailer and put cardboard in his shoes to cover the holes now controls a company with revenues of $500 million a year. His wife, Linda, is president and CEO of the Stamford, Conn., corporation; their children, Stephanie and Shane, both work for the company; and the whole family appears in the shows. His kids are so devoted that Shane McMahon even asked his father to be his best man at his wedding a few years ago.

Linda likes to tell the story of when Shane was 4 years old and was terrified one night that Dracula was hiding in the closet. No amount of reassurance by his mother could change his mind. Finally, Vince strode into the room, heading right into the closet. After a great deal of crashing and banging, he emerged and closed the door. "You don't have to worry anymore," he assured his son. "Dracula is dead."

As a father, McMahon understood the importance of quieting a child's fears about violence and terror. But a wrestling promoter's job, he tells interviewers, is not that of a parent. So don't expect McMahon to slay one of parents' current nightmares, the sordid spectacle of professional wrestling. That's one monster that he prefers not to see.

2

Professional Wrestling Is Popular Entertainment

Bruce R. Miller

Bruce R. Miller is a managing editor and staff writer for the Sioux City Journal *in Iowa. He writes entertainment stories and is the news journal's movie, music, and theater critic.*

Marketing has changed the face of professional wrestling since its origins in the early 1950s. Agreements once made in smoke-filled rooms are now made with a staff of attorneys. Matches once fought for small stakes have now developed into elaborate productions in a multimillion-dollar industry, and pro wrestlers are now some of the most popular characters on cable television. Promoters no longer care if people realize that pro wrestling is choreographed because fans do not care. Most fans know pro wrestling is entertainment and appreciate modern wrestling's athletic soap opera dramas. The injuries are sometimes real, however, and pro wrestlers must train to avoid injuries.

Sting remembers the day when wrestling had no world order, new or otherwise.

"I used to travel 250, 300 miles one way, every single day of the week to wrestle some idiot for 50 bucks," he says. "Now, we're seen by 40 million people a week and it's high stakes."

So high, in fact, that wrestling routinely holds the top spots in cable television's weekly ratings.

A multi-million dollar business, professional wrestling has drawn interest from all corners of the entertainment industry. Thanks to Jesse Ventura's success in the Minnesota gubernatorial race it has even gotten attention from the folks in politics.

So what makes this generation's wrestlers so different from their predecessors? One word: Marketing.

Thanks to licensing arrangements with toy manufacturers, poster and T-shirt makers, folks like Sting, Bill Goldberg and Hulk Hogan are everywhere. They're hot. They're hip. They're humongous.

For fans, they're living, breathing soap opera actors playing out their dramas in the ultimate theater-in-the-round.

"Most of the people out there truly do realize that the business is choreographed," Goldberg says. "But, then again, I think my character puts a little bit of doubt in their minds."

Because the bumps and bruises are real (ask Goldberg to show you his scars), there's an element of wrestling that's hardly fake.

Some aspects of the game may be "pre-determined," Goldberg says, but they're not fake.

For fans, they're living, breathing soap opera actors playing out their dramas in the ultimate theater-in-the-round.

"Injuries are a big factor in our business," says Eric Bischoff, president of World Championship Wrestling (WCW). "I've got a roster of people right now who are laid up due to the injuries that they sustained in the ring. It's a very, very physical business but it is entertainment. We're not trying to be out there in the forefront of this industry, convincing people that it's real . . . but we're not fake sports."

Goldberg, in fact, learned as much when he made the transition from professional football. "Learning not to hurt people was very difficult, coming from a world where your goal is to take people's heads off every time the ball is snapped. But I've had a fairly extensive background in martial arts and that has helped me quite a bit in sparring with friends of mine. You learn to pull your punches and you learn to go full force. But you learn to do it in a manner to where you really don't hurt the guy because you know he's your friend."

Sting says wrestling can be dirty, even political at times. "But that comes with the territory. Whether you play football like Bill did, basketball, baseball, hockey—it's all the same. It's just higher level now and attorneys are involved. Instead of smoke-filled rooms and secret conversations, now you have an attorney sitting across from you—from entertainment attorneys to criminal attorneys, depending on what the problem is."

Changed fans

Fans, too, have changed.

"Fans today are educated," Sting says. "They know that we are sports entertainment. Ten, 12 years ago when I first started if you mentioned or talked as though wrestling were fake your hands were busted, your legs were busted, you were blackballed from wrestling. It's totally different now."

Because the industry is so big, there's space for every kind of wrestler, every type of fan.

Ric Flair, Bischoff says, "represents a portion of the audience that loves the traditional nature of what we do every week. I represent a segment of the audience looking for something other than what is traditional. So we're just taking those two character qualities and letting them beat the hell out of each other every Monday night."

Because the WCW and the World Wrestling Federation are battling for many of the same viewers, "the bar has been raised in many different ways," Bischoff says. "The most attractive one is the amount of revenue that's been generated by the industry.

"What we do today in the ring is really no different than what this industry has been doing since the early '50s. But what is different is the amount of people watching it and paying attention to it."

Disgruntled wrestlers who have tried to "debunk" the form haven't gotten anywhere, Bischoff says, because fans don't care. "People watch wrestling because they want to be entertained. We create emotion. It's no different than any other form of entertainment."

3

Promoters Control the Fate of Professional Wrestlers

Peter Kafka

Peter Kafka writes articles on contemporary businesspeople and current issues in business for Forbes, *a business and financial news magazine.*

Although professional wrestlers are both showmen and athletes, unlike other entertainers and pro athletes, pro wrestlers have little control over their fate. Promoters determine the roles wrestlers will play, when they will perform, and what percentage of revenues they will receive. Like other pro athletes, wrestlers suffer painful injuries, yet only a select few earn more than a million dollars. Most agree, however, that the business has improved from wrestling's early years, and some pro wrestlers have devised ways to increase their earnings. For example, Stone Cold Steve Austin, portrayed by Steve Williams, frequently changes his catch phrases to boost sales of merchandise, and others have used their fame to obtain film roles.

Steve Williams is six-foot-two, 252 pounds, and has one mean-looking, goateed bowling ball of a head. The 34-year-old professional wrestler performs as "Stone Cold Steve Austin," a beer-guzzling hell-raiser. As the main draw for Titan Sports' World Wrestling Federation, Williams made more than $5 million in 1998 and was one of the hottest stars in entertainment.

But for all his might, he has roughly the same control over his career as Homer Simpson. Titan controls Williams's fate—whom he fights, whether he wins—and it's Titan owner Vince McMahon who arbitrarily determines his weekly bonus. Williams says the Stone Cold persona that sold 12 million T shirts in 1998 is an extension of his own personality. Yet Titan owns the character's trademarks.

It's the very antithesis of what you see in almost any other entertainment venue, where the performer owns the franchise value of celebritydom. "This business right now is a lot like Hollywood in the 1930s and 1940s, when the studios had all the power," says Al Snow, a soft-spoken wrestler for Titan whose gimmick involves toting around a mannequin's severed head. "But I think you could see it evolve the same way, where the stars will have more influence."

Someday, maybe. A longtime denizen of Saturday morning television, wrestling now dominates cable-television ratings and rules the pay-per-view TV market. Titan and its rival, Turner Broadcasting's World Championship Wrestling, each appear to have had revenues of more than $200 million in 1998. The performers don't get very much of that revenue.

Wrestlers sign on as independent contractors to contracts of three to five years. The promoters develop the characters the wrestlers portray, script the story lines and determine exposure. This allows Titan and Turner to cook up stars instantaneously: both Williams and Turner star Bill Goldberg rose from bit players to top-of-the-card status in a matter of months. When the promoters decide their acts are stale, the stars find themselves wrestling at the beginning of shows rather than at the climax, or off the shows altogether.

It's the very antithesis of what you see in almost any other entertainment venue, where the performer owns the franchise value of celebritydom.

Titan and Turner can license the performer's likenesses at will. Want to put Goldberg on a lunchbox? You need approval from Turner.

A handful of wrestlers, like Terry (Hollywood Hogan) Bollea, break the million-dollar-a-year mark, but most of the 150 wrestlers under contract to Turner or Titan get a base salary of $80,000 to $200,000. The lucky ones receive up to one third of the royalties their characters generate from merchandise. Titan wrestlers get a fluctuating weekly bonus.

The performers confront what economists call a duopsony—Turner and Titan are the only buyers. Both shell out just $30 million—15% of revenue—for their talent pool. Compare that with the 48% of revenues that NBA owners pay their players or the $20 million check that Jim Carrey earned for the $60 million flop *The Cable Guy*.

Goldberg, who in 1998 went from anonymous ex-NFL lineman to Turner's brightest star, has a base salary of less than $1 million. He can console himself that Turner is an improvement over wrestling's ramshackle minor leagues, where aspiring stars get $25 a night to fight in high school gyms or National Guard Armories.

And it's better than pro wrestling's old days, when contracts consisted of handshakes and dubious promises to share in the gate with promoters. "We worked out of our shirt pockets," says Ken Patera, who wrestled from 1972 to 1988, often at the top of the card. At his peak, Patera would gross $140,000 a year and net $42,000 after travel, medical and legal expenses.

The characteristics of a pro wrestler

The average wrestler can fight more than 180 times a year, and the outings take a physical toll. The matches may be put-ons, but these are still very large men colliding into each other. Guys routinely perform with broken ribs or dislocated thumbs. A wrestler who's done his job well ends the night feeling as if he's played a full-contact football game.

"You're not totally comfortable with it," says wrestler Snow, "but you accept certain givens when you get into this business."

"I'm a good candidate for a knee replacement," says Williams, who has wrestled for nine years. He now saves certain crowd-pleasing, body-abusing moves—absorbing a pile driver, leaping off the top rope—for showcase events. But a certain amount of pain comes with the territory: Snow is wrestling with a fractured right arm.

Thick skin isn't the only requirement. Wrestlers also need to be great showmen. "Give a good wrestler a microphone, push him out the door, ask him for ten minutes [of ranting and crowd-stirring] and you'll get ten great minutes," says Michael Braverman, Goldberg's Los Angeles-based manager. "Who else can do that?"

Resourceful wrestlers manage to find ways to increase their value. Some cut low-level, car dealership-type deals on their own. Williams changes his T shirt styles and catch-phrases every few months in order to goose merchandise sales. But most wrestlers have a good sense of their place in the economic food chain.

In the meantime some wrestlers are already trying to parlay their fame into acting roles that don't involve tights. Williams appeared in CBS's *Nash Bridges,* and Goldberg plays a villain opposite Jean-Claude Van Damme in the film *Universal Soldier II.*

And Goldberg has a good chance at a second film. He's auditioning for a role in a made-for-TV movie: the life story of Minnesota Governor Jesse (The Body) Ventura.

4

Professional Wrestling Is Violent and Sexually Explicit

David Holmstrom

David Holmstrom is a senior feature writer for the Christian Science Monitor, *a national daily newspaper. Holmstrom writes about social issues, criminal justice, education, and entertainment.*

While fans appreciate the well-crafted dramas and superb athleticism of professional wrestling, many authorities feel that professional wrestling programs are unsuitable for children and teenagers. Critics claim these programs—with their emphasis on confrontation and disrespect—reflect contemporary society's distorted values. Pro wrestling no longer pits good guys against bad guys. In today's wrestling matches, everyone is a bad guy, and fans root for their favorite antihero. Some argue these antiheroes place too much emphasis on violence and sex. In the fight for TV ratings, however, the two major wrestling organizations have adopted a "top this" philosophy, increasing the hostility and sexual themes. Despite criticism of the industry, fans continue to support pro wrestling, and promoters continue to meet the demand.

A round me is a sellout crowd of 19,000 roaring, screaming fans in Boston's Fleet Center. In the ring is wrestling's current megastar, a 252-pound nihilist bruiser known as Stone Cold Steve Austin. He is body slamming The Rock, a 275-pound muscled fireplug who wants us to believe he is groggy from the punishment.

He isn't, but in the flip-flop reality of wrestling, fans love the exaggerated show of clashing bodies. It's as if a comic strip or Saturday-morning cartoon has come to life. They are believers in the crunching reality of wrestling's make-believe.

The crowd noise reaches maximum volume as Stone Cold continues to treat The Rock like a rag doll. But beneath the noise in the arena, and the skyrocketing popularity of wrestling across the United States, questions about wrestling's atmosphere and social impact won't go away.

For instance, in Row J, just behind me, a man wearing a T-shirt proclaiming the virtues of a sand-blasting company is on his feet bellowing obscenities at Stone Cold. His one digit gesture joins a forest of one-digit gestures all around us.

Seated next to him is an eight- or nine-year-old boy, eyes wide, his left thumb in his mouth. His right hand has pulled the long sleeve of his shirt over his left hand and thumb in an attempt to hide his thumb-sucking.

Here in the midst of the World Wrestling Federation's (WWF) scripted, multimillion-dollar, body-slamming entertainment event, a small boy and his thumb suggest the runaway popularity of wrestling is not for him.

A new emphasis on hostility, obscenity, and sex

Many child experts would agree: Much of today's wrestling presented by the WWF and World Championship Wrestling (WCW) has a newfound emphasis on hostility, obscenities, and sexual explicitness.

They say it is unsuitable for young children and even 13- and 14-year-olds. While most adults know the matches are scripted, children, with less experience and judgment, see the conflicts and concocted violence differently. The wrestlers consider themselves skillful athlete-entertainers, not involved in "fakery" because injuries do occur.

Still, the majority of the audience in the Fleet Center is young men in their early 20s, teens, and preteens (many in groups and brought in by adults). The taunting hostility flows among the wrestlers, and back and forth from wrestlers to fans, some of it done with laughter.

But all this has changed the previous good guy vs. bad guy roles that prevailed in wrestling from the 1940s to the late 1980s.

Mike Shadow, who paid $30 each for himself and his 12-year-old son for seats at the Fleet, is asked if this is a good atmosphere for his son. "Not really," he says, "if we're talking about a moral standpoint. Wrestling has changed since I was a kid, the language and the themes. But listen, there is a lot worse sexual stuff on TV, and he hears a lot worse than this at school. For me, it's how you interpret all this to him."

While most adults know the matches are scripted, children, with less experience and judgment, see the . . . concocted violence differently.

Some child experts see wrestling's values reflecting some of society's distorted values. "Our culture has become one of confrontation and disrespect," says Michael Brody, a child psychiatrist at the Media Committee of the American Academy of Child and Adolescent Psychiatry in Washington. "And wrestling fits [with] what has happened in our culture. It's entertainment today. It's the Jerry Springer Show with physical action."

Hulk Hogan, now known as Hollywood Hulk Hogan, was wrestling's fair-haired boy in the 1980s when he was the megastar "good guy" wrestler. But in a shift of character roles, just before his alleged retirement from wrestling, he became mean and taunting in his matches. "Everybody in wrestling today is really a bad guy," explains David Lenker, editor-in-chief of *The Wrestler* magazine. "The issue is which bad guys are popular and which bad guys are hated. And it has a lot to do with the fact that everybody has an attitude, and it's the tough-talking guys with a lot of personality that appeal to a lot of people."

A battle for wrestling's millions

What has fed the character change is the rivalry between the WCW and WWF, the two leading promoters of wrestling in the US. Each organization has a stable of wrestlers pretending to be constantly and publicly at war with each other and their bosses, Vince McMahon, the president of WWF, and Eric Bischoff, the president of WCW.

Some child experts see wrestling's values reflecting some of society's distorted values.

At stake is millions of dollars. "These two companies are at war for TV ratings, merchandising, everything," Mr. Lenker says. "Just about everybody believes that WCW has the stronger talent roster from top to bottom such as Goldberg [285 pounds], Kevin Nash [367 pounds], Scott Hall, and Ric Flair." But the WWF has Stone Cold, Undertaker (328 pounds), Kane (326 pounds), and a female wrestler named Sable, all of whom are well-known in households that follow wrestling.

Every Monday night on cable television, the two organizations square off in prime time. WWF's "Raw Is War" starts at 9 P.M. on the USA Network, and WCW's "Monday Nitro" airs at 8 P.M. on TNT. Both shows, before huge crowds in different cities each week, feature rock music, fireworks, dancing girls, and soap-opera-like chapters in well-crafted, loud-mouthed rivalries among the wrestlers. Often, the huge bodies tumble out of the ring and carry on their pseudobattles three feet from the clamoring crowd.

Both shows usually sit atop the cable ratings for Monday night, attracting a combined audience of 10 million viewers. *TV Guide* says the wrestling audience was 36 percent larger in 1998 than 1997. WCW reports that 25 percent of its audience are kids and teens ranging from age 2 to 17, and 50 percent are men 18 and over. It was this latter demographic, as voters, that helped elect former wrestler Jesse Ventura governor of Minnesota.

The wrestling shows are heavy with commercials, many promoting violent video games along with Wendy's, Chevrolet, or movies from Warner Bros, Sony, or Miramax. On a recent Monday night, the "Nitro" show carried 103 commercials in two hours.

"WWF has been allowed by USA Network to make its program more adult-oriented with [strong] language and sexually oriented themes," Lenker says, "and TNT, through Time Warner and Ted Turner, has tried to make 'Nitro' more family-oriented." But both shows are long rumbles of hostility, devoid of humor, unless one regards them as a kind of unintentional satire on male bravado.

Les Thatcher, who was a popular wrestler in the US from 1960 to 1979 and now operates the Main Event Pro Wrestling Camp in Cincinnati, has mixed emotions about wrestling's new attitude, and suggests that if it escalates it might eventually trigger a decline.

"I'm not personally offended by some of the sexual stuff," he says, "but I'm looking at the 17,000 people in the building, and the kids under 10, and I'm wondering how many mothers and fathers are offended? These are ticket buyers, and is this some cheap shot to them? I've been in wrestling 39 years, and now the business is so good we think we can't make any mistakes.

"I think we're about two years away from making big mistakes if we continually play, 'Can you top this?' with the sex and language stuff."

For now, the fans are still lining up. At one of the merchandising counters at the Fleet Center, they were 10 deep buying T-shirts, big foam hands forming an obscene gesture, plastic championship belts, hats, plastic figures of wrestlers, videos, CDs, and more.

"I find wrestling tremendously entertaining," says Chuck Green, an accountant with Ben and Jerry's, the ice creammakers, while buying a hot dog at the Fleet Center. "It's the best theatrics I've ever seen. I have a master's degree in business, and all my associates think I'm crazy, but to me it's great."

5

Professional Wrestling Contributes to America's Culture of Violence

Ted Rueter

Ted Rueter is a professor of political science at the University of California at Los Angeles. Rueter writes books and articles on political behavior and public opinion, appears on radio talk shows, and has been involved in several political campaigns.

Filled with violence, vulgarity, and simulated sex, professional wrestling programs have become part of America's culture of violence. Today's pro wrestling matches are not only violent and obscene, but demeaning to women. Even some pro wrestlers believe the business is a disgrace. In light of overwhelming evidence that violent entertainment causes violent behavior, many authorities are disturbed that professional wrestling appeals to adolescent boys who are already prone to aggression. Some teens imitate the violence they see in dangerous backyard wrestling matches. Pro wrestling is also dangerous for the wrestlers themselves; several have even died performing dangerous stunts. Unfortunately, corporate America supports the violence and sexual themes in order to cash in on wrestling's popularity.

The shootings at schools in Colorado, Georgia, and Oklahoma have reenergized the debate over juvenile crime. Pundits and politicians have pointed to guns, R-rated movies, violent video games, Marilyn Manson concerts, and family breakdown as causes of America's culture of violence.

I have another pernicious force to suggest: professional wrestling. The epitome of violence, sadomasochism, and sleaze, professional wrestling is trash TV for ugly Americans.

Wrestling is big business. Ted Turner's World Championship Wrestling (WCW) is on TBS and TNT. Vince McMahon's World Wrestling Federation (WWF) is on the USA Network. The WCW reaches an average of 300,000 viewers for its pay-per-view events. The WWF is building a 1,000-room casino hotel in Las Vegas. Both groups sell action figures, neckties, and greeting cards. Two WWF wrestlers—"Mankind" and "The Rock"—currently have best-selling autobiographies. Vince McMahon just announced the formation of a professional football league, the XFL, which will debut in 2001.*

In August 1999, Jesse Ventura, the Governor of Minnesota, stepped back into the ring as a "guest referee" for the WWF's *Summerslam*. He made $1 to $2 million on video sales and the use of his name.

And now yet another professional wrestler is entering the political ring. WCW star Rik Flair has announced that he's running for governor of North Carolina.

Professional wrestling is obscene

Wrestlers pumped up on steroids use all sorts of great moves—eye gouges, smashing chairs, low blows, choke holds, body slams, crude gestures, and crass banter—to the background of fireworks and dazzling lights. In a recent broadcast, a wrestler was hung on a cross. "Stone Cold" Steve Austin—the top attraction of the WWF—is best known for extending his middle finger during matches and interviews.

Walter Gantz, a professor of telecommunication studies at Indiana University, analyzed 50 episodes of *WWF Raw* between January 12, 1998 and February 1, 1999. He found hundreds of instances of crude remarks, vulgar gestures, Satanic activity, and simulated drug use and sexual activity.

Wrestling is overtly misogynist. Between matches, scantily-clad women parade around the ring. Women grapplers are subject to "after-hours wrestling" (a version of the Hollywood casting couch). Sable, wrestling's biggest female star, recently settled a lawsuit against the WWF, in which she alleged that the business "had become so obscene and so vulgar" that she no longer wishes to be a part of it.

The epitome of violence, sadomasochism, and sleaze, professional wrestling is trash TV for ugly Americans.

Another obscenity is the danger faced by wrestlers. At least 20 professional wrestlers have died in the last five years from wrestling injuries. On May 23, 1999, Owen Hart fell 90 feet to his death from a rafter in a Kansas City arena, before 16,000 screaming fans. After Hart's body was moved from the ring, the promoter decided that the show must go on!

Martha Hart, Owen's widow, has initiated a 46-count lawsuit against the WWF, contending that "professional wrestling has become a showy display of graphic violence, sexual themes, and dangerous stunts."

Unfortunately, many adolescent boys are imitating these behaviors. Nationwide, teens are staging wrestling matches in their back yards, complete with the pile drivers and sexual innuendo they see on television.

* The XFL debuted in 2001 but disbanded after one season.

There are backyard wrestling groups in 30 states. The Backyard Wrestling Federation broadcast teen matches through its web site until it was closed down in July 1999 because of liability concerns.

A destructive influence

The behavior of teen wrestling fans is not surprising. There have been 1,000 published reports on the impact of TV violence. The National Institute of Mental Health says there is overwhelming evidence that violent entertainment causes violent behavior. For example, homicide rates doubled within 15 years after television was introduced into specific areas of the United States and Canada.

Professional wrestling is a destructive influence on adolescent boys—who already face trouble. Harvard Medical School professor William Pollack, author of *Real Boys*, argues that today's young males are prone to depression, isolation, despair, and aggression. According to Pollack, today's young males suffer increasing rates of attention-deficit disorder, school absenteeism, psychiatric disorders, and suicide.

Corporate America is in bed with professional wrestling. Burger King, Western Union, Gatorade, and Universal Studios all advertise on the Monday night WWF show. There were sex-saturated ads for wrestling during 1999's Super Bowl. Little Caesar's latest ads have a wrestling theme. Ted Turner—the man who gave a billion dollars to the United Nations and shows *Andy Griffith* re-runs—has sold his soul for wrestling cash. Commendably, Coca-Cola recently severed its relationship with the WWF.

As a child growing up in Minnesota, I was a big fan of the local wrestling show. Every Saturday night at 6:30, I watched WTCN's matches from the Calhoun Beach Club. I remember Verne Gagne, the Crusher, the Bruiser, and Dr. X competing for the "world championship" of the metropolitan mosquito control district. The studio was the size of a garage. There were no crazed crowds. There were no wild stunts. There were no nearly-naked women.

I saw another wrestling old-timer, Mad Dog Vachon, at a fair. The veteran of 13,000 matches, Mad Dog was charming and amusing. He also commented that contemporary wrestling is a "complete disgrace."

A few months ago, the "V-chip" was introduced into all new television sets in America, designed to block out violent programming. What we need now is the "W-chip."

6

Professional Wrestling Has a Negative Impact on Young People

Walt Mueller

Walt Mueller is a youth ministry specialist who teaches courses on youth ministry and culture at Geneva College in Beaver Falls, Pennsylvania. Mueller has written several books, including Understanding Today's Youth Culture, *and is founder of the Center for Parent/Youth Understanding (CPYU).*

Professional wrestling is a pervasive cultural phenomenon that dominates cable TV ratings and appeals to an increasingly wider audience. However, the content of pro wrestling has changed. Rather than root for the good guy over the bad guy, today's pro wrestling audience cheers for its favorite "heel." The athleticism and drama of pro wrestling are entertaining and provide fans a way to vent their anger. Unfortunately, pro wrestling also reflects an ideology of moral chaos that is being marketed to young children. Rather than forbid children from watching pro wrestling, parents should ask why their children become interested in its violent and vengeful world and, if necessary, offer alternative models to resolve conflict. Parents should also discourage their children from watching pro wrestling matches and should refuse to support the industry by watching themselves.

It was our inability to keep from crossing the thin line between fiction and reality that forced our mother to declare a halt to the playful sibling scuffles we initiated on the living room carpet and front lawn. We were three young brothers who had accumulated an arsenal of eye-pokes, boinks, and other "yuk-yuk" moves from hours spent watching *The Three Stooges*. Our all-too-real imitation gradually led to maternal intervention and the elimination of Moe, Larry, and Curley (or sometimes Shemp) from our TV diet.

Banned from the Stooges, it wasn't long before we discovered a tele-

From "My Week in Professional Wrestling," by Walt Mueller, CPYU Newsletter, Winter 1999. Copyright © 1999 by the Center for Parent/Youth Understanding, www.cpyu.org. Reprinted with permission.

vised substitute for the Stooges that took our grappling sessions to new heights of frenzied fun. We would spend time on Saturdays soaking up one of the many benefits of boyhood in the suburbs of Philadelphia—professional wrestling televised on a local UHF station! All of a sudden, our savage repertoire expanded to include pile drivers, leg drops, eye-gouges, sleeper holds, and the always lethal "hidden foreign object." It didn't matter that we could never seem to figure out if what we were watching was fake or real. We were now imitating the likes of Chief Jay Strongbow, Bruno Sammartino, "Polish Power" Ivan Putski, and Gorilla Monsoon. Sadly, mom would often intervene and end our bouts with a reprimand that served as a quick bell. Admittedly, our "professional" matches sometimes degenerated quickly into something much too real.

I don't remember when I lost my childhood fascination with professional wrestling. Maybe it was when I grew up a little and finally realized it was all staged. After all, people usually feel cheated when they find out they've wasted valuable time on something "fake" or "fixed"—right? Not always. Judging from the mounting popularity of professional wrestling among children, teens, and adults of all ages, that certainly isn't the case anymore.

Wrestling is everywhere

Wrestling occupies a growing spot on the cultural landscape. Live venues in cities across North America are sold out every night. Not a day seems to go by when you can't find wrestling somewhere on the TV. Billed as nothing more or less than "sports entertainment" (another way of saying "fake"), professional wrestling is pervasive.

During the last two or three years, my frequent episodes of channel-surfing to catch the latest in pop culture have included a growing number of glimpses into the wrestling world. It's not the world I remember from my childhood. But it appears to be a big part of the entertainment diet of today's children, teens, *and* a significant number of adults. Because of this, it's time to take a deeper look at the world of professional wrestling. What is it all about? Why is it so popular? Is it harmless entertainment or something more?

Not a day seems to go by when you can't find wrestling somewhere on the TV.

Because parents, educators, and youth workers need to know more about this powerful cultural force, I decided to go back into professional wrestling. For one week in September 1999, I hunkered down and watched every minute of televised wrestling available where I live. Then I read everything written about wrestling I could get my hands on. I came away with a spinning head and two conclusions. First, my mother would be appalled if her three boys started imitating today's pro grapplers. And second, watching wrestling was an exercise in cultural education.

In a cover article on the professional wrestling phenomenon, *Entertainment Weekly* called it "the hottest, most innovative entertainment pop culture has to offer." (*Entertainment Weekly*, 4/16/99). The numbers support that opinion.

Most televised wrestling events feature the two major rival wrestling organizations: The World Wrestling Federation (WWF) and World Championship Wrestling (WCW). Thanks to effective marketing, the sport has become the highest rated programming on cable TV. The two tours produce over 15 hours of weekly programming watched by over 35 million viewers. In all, seven different wrestling programs consistently finish in the top ten cable ratings every week. The WCW beams its programming worldwide. The WWF is translated into 11 languages and can be seen in over 120 countries around the globe. Between 1997 and 1998, the WWF saw a 156 percent ratings rise among viewers with four or more years of college, and a 111 percent rise in households with incomes of $50,000 or more.

Regular pay-per-view events give viewers even more options. Add these revenues to the sales of wrestling merchandise (trading cards, shirts, hats, videos, magazines, lunch boxes, action figures, toys, music compilation CDs, and everything else imaginable), and it's clear why revenues are so high! The WWF sold over $1 billion in merchandise during 1998. That figure could double in 1999. [In May 1999, wrestling toy sales were up 389 percent over the same period in 1998.] According to one report, the professional wrestling business grossed only $100,000 less than major league baseball in 1998. Maybe it's not surprising that 96 percent of the top 1000 sports sites on the web are devoted to wrestling (*Spin*, 12/98).

Whatever happened to "the good old days?"

For years, the world of professional wrestling provided morality plays (yes, they were staged) on the never-ending struggle between good and evil. Night after night in dimly lit arenas across the country, fans gathered to cheer for "the babyface" as he (or sometimes she) would enter the ring to defend honor against "the heel." Fans would cheer as the modest and soft-spoken "face" would never stray from the bounds of fighting with fairness. The evil, loud-mouthed, and arrogant heel, often representing enemies of the United States (for example, Russian wrestler Ivan Koloff during the Cold War, complete with a sickle and hammer tattoo), would resort to the use of any illegal tactic (eye-poking, kicking, hair-pulling, choking, etc.) in order to gain the upper-hand. The heel was often accompanied by a flamboyant manager who served as an accomplice, distracting the referee so they could inflict more underhanded damage to the babyface.

Today, that's all changed. Good and evil no longer do battle in the ring. Instead, wrestling is a never-ending melodramatic soap opera where complex storylines run from week to week as evil battles evil. Today's wrestling audience cheers for decadence doing battle with decadence. It's "heel" versus "heel." The wrestling world runs on the fuel of vulgarity, sexual desire, infidelity, arrogance, rebellion, and attitude. Henry Jenkins, Professor of Comparative Media Studies at MIT and author of a book on wrestling, says wrestling is "a morally ambiguous universe, with antiheros and sympathetic villains." (*US News & World Report*, 5/17/99).

This rapid shift in emphasis is best evidenced in the moral metamorphosis of Hulk Hogan, maybe the most popular wrestler of the past 15 or 20 years. In the 80s "the Hulkster" was the WWF's superhero good guy who loved the millions of kids who loved him. Since moving to the WCW in 1994, bad guy "Hollywood Hogan" became the leader of the "New World Order," a group of rebel wrestlers intent on ousting the head of their TV network, Ted Turner. "Now I'm the worst bad guy around," he says. "I can't win a match unless I cheat. And people love me." (*Time*, 6/29/98). It was a move he needed to make to ensure continued popularity. Since then the entire world of wrestling has followed the Hulkster's lead.

An in-depth look at the more recent history of professional wrestling offers further insight into its changing nature and subsequent popularity in today's youth culture.

The world of wrestling today

The common thread of wrestling past and wrestling present is that the combatants are usually massive and muscular men (and women!) who enter the ring to perform elaborately scripted encounters full of acrobatic moves, fake punches, emphatic grunts, and an endless parade of "near-falls" (two-counts that end before a pin as the helpless loser gains a sudden burst of energy in time to escape defeat). It's there the comparison ends.

Today's televised wrestling opens with the fanfare of loud heavy metal music and cutting edge graphics. After these intros, the camera zooms in, on and around an arena full of frenzied fans (many of them young children—some on their Dad's shoulders) who have assembled to scream for their heroes. Elaborate staging, state-of-the-art lighting effects, huge video screens, fireworks, and rock music combine to set the tone and leave viewers with the sense that something exciting is about to happen.

Part of the show themselves, the fans sport painted faces, wrestling T-shirts, and home-made signs. Television viewers will notice immediately that many of the signs display profanity and a variety of other vulgarities. On one episode of *WCW Monday Night Nitro*, the camera caught signs with the messages "Fah-Q" and "I raped Nitro Girl" (the name for the WCW's group of girl dancers).

> *The wrestling world runs on the fuel of vulgarity, sexual desire, infidelity, arrogance, rebellion, and attitude.*

Each wrestler, with a well-developed and distinctive persona, enters the arena with their own trade-mark entrance while their personal theme-song and video plays. The audience only needs to hear two or three notes and their familiarity with the music lets them know who's coming next. Then the crowd taunts, jeers, or cheers as the wrestler makes his or her way to the ring.

Usually, the fighting begins before the first bell as someone delivers a cheap shot. Rarely does the fighting stay in the ring. It spills out onto the floor, into the audience, and backstage. Of course, the crowd never misses any of it as it's all displayed on big screens in the arena.

The behemoths perform moves with amazing agility and acrobatic precision. Sometimes an accomplice will show up and enter the fight. Foreign objects are no longer hidden. Steel steps, pipes, small appliances, tables, metal folding chairs, trash cans, and a variety of other objects are used as weapons. Their use elicits a thunderous roar from the crowd. After numerous near-falls and nick-of-time escapes, one of the wrestlers will execute their patented personal "finishing move," usually ending the match. The crowd goes nuts.

But that's only the wrestling. The majority of the broadcast and live arena event centers on the ongoing soap operas working themselves out between wrestling's colorful cast of characters. It's a world of constantly shifting allegiance, harassment, posturing, betrayal, and the quest for one of the many available title belts. The major wrestling federations actually employ writers to develop the elaborate story lines. As silly as it sounds, all this combines to create an adrenaline rush that's fast, furious, and leaves fans hungering for more.

The man behind the new face of wrestling

Any history of the changing face of wrestling must start with the man most responsible for these changes, Vince McMahon, Jr. The fifty-three year-old McMahon has been around wrestling his entire life. His grandfather, Jess McMahon, ran the Capital Wrestling Federation in the Northeast. Father Vince, Sr. took over and renamed the organization the World Wide Wrestling Federation. In 1982, Vince, Jr. bought out his father and assumed control of the operation, renaming it the World Wrestling Federation.

One of his first moves was to de-regionalize professional wrestling. Until that time each area of the country had its own federation with its own stars, audience, circuits, "world champions," and local television contract. Like a rich man playing Monopoly, McMahon quickly bought them up and with the purchase of Georgia Championship Wrestling in 1984, the WWF was now national.

An imaginative showman, McMahon quickly developed a new set of rules with extreme personalities and ongoing story lines. Andre the Giant and Hulk Hogan were the wrestlers used to build the empire. Knowing that rock-n-roll concerts were selling out arenas, McMahon injected a heavy dose of rock-n-roll into wrestling with the sets, loud music, lighting, elaborate costumes, and face-painting. This exciting new brand of wrestling found a rapidly growing audience around the world—particularly among children and teens who loved their rock music. A series of pay-per-view "Wrestlemania" events drew huge crowds and pay-per-view audiences, with over 93,000 attending 1987's "Wrestlemania III" at the Pontiac Silverdome.

As the story goes, the WWF's main rival, World Championship Wrestling, came into existence after media mogul Ted Turner tried to purchase the WWF from McMahon. The WWF was getting high ratings on Turner's TBS network and Turner wanted to get into the action. When McMahon refused to sell, Turner proceeded to buy out a number of independent regional wrestling federations spread across the south. The WCW was born and debuted on TBS in 1991.

Not only did McMahon now have competition, but he and his WWF ran into other trouble during the early 90s. The WWF nearly went under after McMahon was indicted on charges of distributing and abusing steroids, as well as sexual harassment. Eventually McMahon was acquitted in 1994 but the damage had been done. The WCW had hired away WWF stars Ric Flair, Hulk Hogan, and Kevin Nash. Overall television ratings fell and attendance at live events was cut in half.

But just like the two-count near-falls in which an unconscious wrestler springs back to new life, Vince McMahon jumped up off the mat with a two-part formula that's brought wrestling to its new heights of popularity.

First, he took "successful" elements of pop culture and injected them into his WWF world. "The WWF is a soap, it's an action adventure, it's a live-action cartoon, and it's part talk show," says McMahon. "A hybrid of everything successful on TV, all rolled into one." (*Entertainment Weekly,* 4/16/99). In another interview, McMahon told *Time,* "We're storytellers. You just can't throw wrestlers out there to wrestle. That's not what an audience wants to see." (6/29/98). The stories have become so much a part of the show, that actual in-ring wrestling occurs during only about 25 percent of a WWF broadcast.

And second, he removed any and all rules of decency that might have still been there. The result—decadence and moral chaos. An Indiana University study of 50 episodes of the Monday night *WWF Raw* broadcasts from 1998 found the following: 1,658 incidents of a character grabbing or pointing to their own crotch (not counting the slow-motion instant replays), 157 instances of wrestlers or audience members making an obscene gesture; 434 times people either said a sexually charged slogan or displayed one on a sign; 128 episodes of simulated sexual activity; 47 references to Satanic activity; and 609 instances of wrestlers or others being struck by objects like garbage cans or nightsticks.

"The WWF is a soap, it's an action adventure, it's a live-action cartoon, and it's part talk show," says [Vince] McMahon.

In September 1998, the Parents Television Council conducted an analysis of the WWF's Thursday night broadcast of *Smackdown.* They concluded that the most shocking feature was the obscenity with 25 incidents of foul language per hour. Judging from what I saw during one week, 1999 is even worse.

George magazine reported that wrestling is about one "overriding and inescapable theme . . . transgression. Everywhere one looks in wrestling, someone is crossing the line, challenging the authorities, acting outrageously, disregarding taste and moral tradition. Good and bad have no place in this corrupt universe. Only outlawry does." (7/99). What does Vince McMahon have to say about all this? "I've stopped being (TV's) conscience or policeman. I've adopted the same philosophy as Hollywood: here it is—do you like it or not?" (*Newsweek,* 11/23/98).

With McMahon's question in mind, I hunkered down in front of the television set on a quest to learn not only about professional wrestling, but to discover why so many in our culture do, in fact, like it.

Including pay-per-view, broadcast, and cable shows, I was treated to about 20 hours of wrestling from the WWF, WCW, and ECW (Extreme

Championship Wrestling). The sensory blast, plotlines, vast cast of characters, and overall moral tone left my head spinning.

The WWF

My week began with the WWF—the federation currently boasting the biggest audience, highest TV ratings, highest revenues, and sleaziest cast of characters. During the week I watched, the WWF aired nine hours worth of programming. The most popular WWF prime-time broadcast is *Monday Night Raw*. On Thursdays, fans get another two-hour dose on *WWF Smackdown*. For those trying to keep up with the comings and goings of their WWF heroes, the federation sponsors two one-hour weekly reviews on Saturday and Sunday mornings: *WWF Livewire* and *WWF Superstars*. In addition, I forked out $29.95 to be part of an audience of millions watching the three hour pay-per-view *Unforgiven* sponsored by "Magic–The Gathering" fantasy cards.

No-holds barred sexuality is a big part of WWF character personas.

The fast-paced WWF overload included highly touted matches labeled with all kinds of sad, yet often comical names: The Kennel from Hell Match, The Choke Slam Challenge, The Inferno Match (inside a ring of fire), Hell in a Cell (where the object is to escape the ring and climb over a fence guarded by vicious Rottweilers), the Casket Match (where the winner must drop his opponent in a casket and slam the lid shut), Brahma Bull Rope Match (where the opponents are tied together), and Boiler Room Brawl (an anything goes contest in the arena's boiler room).

One of the most unbelievable matches on *Raw* was The Evening Gown Match—just one example of how the WWF capitalizes on sexual desire and the bizarre. Wrestling old-timers The Fabulous Moolah and May Young (over 70 years old!) took on Ivory—one of the WWF's large-breasted and scantily clad young female sex symbols. As with the WWF's other well-endowed women (Miss Kitty, Debra, etc.), the crowd and announcers continually call for Ivory to "show your puppies" (breasts). The object of the match—to strip your opponent down to their undergarments. Ivory was only able to strip May Young down to her bra and panties before Moolah was successful at doing the same to Ivory, who left the ring defeated and wearing only a scanty bra and thong for the entire cheering audience to see. Of course, the WWF's TV announcers add a heavy dose of straightforward sexual commentary and double-meanings throughout the match and the entire show.

One wonders how long it will be before the TV audience gets to see full-frontal nudity. In one female mud-wrestling match I watched, the two well-endowed combatants entered the ring in bikinis. The winner left the ring holding the other's bikini top. Although the loser was covered with a thin layer of watery mud, the camera caught a front-shot of her exposed breasts. By the way, this was on regular cable and the live audience was filled with kids.

No-holds barred sexuality is a big part of WWF character personas. Val Venis (rhymes with "penis"), an adult film star, bases his character on the size of his genitalia and is also known as "The Big Ballbowski." He comes to the ring wrapped in a towel and brags about the size of his penis. Recently, he showed the audience a preview of his pornographic film, *Saving Ryan's Privates.*

The Godfather, decked out as a stereotypical 70s pimp, lives by his slogan "Pimpin' ain't easy" and finishes off his opponents with a move called the Pimp Drop. He always enters the ring surrounded by his "ho's" (slang for "whores"), also known as his "ho train."

Al Snow enters the ring carrying a severed woman's head (not real, of course) and wearing a T-shirt emblazoned with a phrase promoting oral sex—"Everyone needs a little head." Upon Snow's arrival in the ring, the announcer asks the audience, "What does everybody need?" and "What does everybody want?" The audience screams the answer to both in unison—"Head!"

I saw an endless parade of sexually suggestive behavior and heard tons of profanity.

One of the most frenzied and super-charged moments of every WWF broadcast is the arrival of the New Age Outlaws into the arena. The tag-team pair (members of the WWF association known as D-Generation X) combines the smart-alec smile of Mr. Ass and the tough-guy talk of the Road Dogg. When their theme music starts, the crowd goes nuts. As they enter the ring, the cheering crowd yells along with the Road Dogg, "Oh you didn't know? Your ass better call somebody!" He then drops the mike to his crotch and simulates sex. The two strut to the ring and the Road Dogg goes through another lengthy recitation that the crowd yells right with him. He often refers to wrestling "Doggy-style." When behind his opponent he sometimes simulates canine intercourse. Once the Road Dogg's done with the mike, he hands it over to Mr. Ass who leads the crowd in a unison yell of the two words most often heard from a WWF crowd—"If you're not down with that, we've got two words for ya—SUCK IT!" The two words serve as the official slogan of D-Generation X. Another member of D-X, the wrestler known as X-Pac, accentuates the slogan by thrusting his pelvis forward and making an "X" across his inner thighs with two karate chops.

Prince Albert, one of the most colorful wrestlers in the WWF, has been labeled the "human pincushion" because of the numerous piercings on his body. His wrestling name comes from the name for a penis piercing—a "Prince Albert."

The sexual antics carry over into the soap opera story lines as wrestlers fight for the right to the tour's female stars. On one broadcast, 380 pound Mark "Sexual Chocolate" Henry stood in the ring and cried to the audience about his "sexual addiction": "I get on base more times than Mark McGwire and Sammy Sosa combined." It's all part of the show and the story line will be continued in future WWF episodes.

Spiritual darkness enters the ring with the arrival of The Undertaker.

Also called "The Lord of Darkness," The Undertaker is known to carry his victims off to be unwilling participants in Satanic rituals. The tag team pair of The Acolytes sport wrestling tights emblazoned with pentagrams.

The importance of attitude

The WWF is permeated with vulgarity. *U.S. News & World Report* says that past episodes of the WWF's broadcasts "have featured mock crucifixions, S&M scenes, wrestlers mooning the audience and each other, and a woman sucking suggestively on an Italian sausage." (5/17/99). As I watched, I saw an endless parade of sexually suggestive behavior and heard tons of profanity with the most popular words being "son of a bitch," "damn," "ass," "balls," and "hell." The WWF is all about attitude. And no two wrestlers provide evidence of that attitude more than the WWF's current most popular pair, The Rock and Stone Cold Steve Austin.

The Rock, known as "The People's Champion," is a third-generation professional wrestler. Born Dwayne Johnson, The Rock grew up watching his grandfather wrestle as "High Chief" Peter Maivia. His father, Rocky Johnson, won the WWF tag-team championship with Tony Atlas in 1983. After a sensational football career as a High-School All-American and defensive lineman at the University of Miami, Dwayne entered the WWF in 1996 as Rocky Maivia. Even though he soon won the Intercontinental Championship Belt, Rocky was too good a guy to warrant continued popularity. He changed his image from "face" to "heel" and has been popular ever since. A master at working up the crowd with the microphone, The Rock has developed patented sayings the crowd anticipates hearing and repeating at every match. Along with his famous raised eyebrow and "The Rock Bottom" finishing move, The Rock is known to never be at a loss for words. He asks the crowd, "Can you smellllllllllllllll what the Rock's got cookin'?" And whether his opponent is carrying a nightstick, metal chair, or any other object, The Rock whips the crowd into a frenzy by telling his nemesis of the moment that he's going to "shine up" the object, "turn that son-of-a-bitch sideways, and stick it up your roody-poo candy ass!"

From the television, to school halls, to store aisles, to the streets—professional wrestling's presence on merchandise is inescapable.

Even though he's not known as "The People's Champion," 33-year old Stone Cold Steve Austin is by far the most popular and revered hero in professional wrestling today. Also known as "The Rattlesnake," Austin's likeness, sayings, and emblems can be found on the 12 million Stone Cold T-shirts sold during 1998. Born Steve Anderson in Texas and abandoned by his biological father, this former college football player was working on the loading docks when he decided to attend a wrestling school. Named "Steve Austin" by another more experienced wrestler, he worked his way around local wrestling circuits for little pay and no recognition. After switching his role from babyface to heel, things got better. Signed in 1991

as "Stunning Steve Austin" by the WCW, he became one of the most popular wrestlers in that organization. A severe tricep injury in 1994 led to his
firing by the WCW. After a brief stint in the ECW, Austin signed a 1995
deal with the WWF and appeared as "the million-dollar champion, The
Ringmaster." The act never really caught on. Inspiration for change came
one night while Austin was watching an HBO film about serial killer
Richard Kuklinski who was nicknamed "The Ice Man." Austin says his new
idea was of "this cold-blooded bastard guy, kinda ruthless, who didn't give
a damn." The WWF liked the idea and gave Austin a three-page list of tem-
perature based names, none of which he liked. Then, while waiting for a
cup of hot tea to cool, Austin's wife told him to hurry up and drink it before it turned "stone cold." He had his name.

Today, Austin struts to the ring with a scowl on his face and lots of
bad attitude while his theme song, "Hell Frozen Over," fills the arena. He
doesn't hesitate to raise his middle fingers at his opponents or the audience. The more antisocial and rebellious he gets, the more the crowd
loves him. Even though the audience loves him, they will often-times
give him the finger right back. He threatens to serve up a "can of 100 percent whoop-ass" on his opponents and tells them he'll force them to
drink "a cup of shut-the-hell-up." After a match, he stands in the ring and
guzzles beer. He's an individual who makes his own rules and plays the
game the same way. Why? The crowd will tell you as they repeat one of
his most famous lines: "Because Stone Cold said so!"

On June 23, 1996, Austin beat Bible-quoting Jake "The Snake"
Roberts. As he stood over the fallen Roberts, Austin made a proclamation
that's plastered all over T-shirts and fan signs as "Austin 3:16": "You
thump your Bible and talk about John 3:16. But Austin 3:16 says I JUST
WHOOPED YOUR ASS!" The crowd went crazy. Stone Cold Steve Austin
embodies the attitude of the WWF.

The WCW

While in the fall of 1999 Ted Turner's WCW was running second in the
ratings and revenue standings, the audience for their three weekly programs was by no means small. Viewers can tune into three hours of *WCW
Monday Nitro*, two hours of *WCW Thunder* on Thursday nights, and another two hours of *WCW Saturday Night* at the end of the week. WCW
also broadcasts a regular schedule of pay-per-view events.

While the WCW relies on the same formula of flamboyant characters
and elaborate melodrama as the WWF, there are some marked differences. The creative forces behind WCW have tried to create a more
"family-friendly" approach to wrestling as they feel the WWF goes too far
with bad taste. What that means is that you won't hear the profanity.
When a wrestler does let it fly, it's usually muted from the broadcast, although I did hear several mentions of "hell," "ass," and "damn." The
"Nitro-Girl" dancers are definitely there for the sex appeal. While the
WCW prides itself on no vulgarities, naked women, or sexual innuendo,
there is certainly enough sexual suggestiveness and in-your-face violence
on the broadcasts. The WCW is actually a toned down WWF featuring a
slate of flamboyant stars including some older WWF castoffs.

When a WCW audience breaks into the chant "Goldberg, Goldberg,

Goldberg," the tour's most famous current star is about to enter the arena. During his trademark entrance he stands in a shower of sparklers, flexes his neck and body, slaps himself, then struts to the ring. His clean-shaven head leaves him looking almost identical to the WWF's Austin. A native of Tulsa, the 284 pound Bill Goldberg was an All-SEC defensive lineman at the University of Georgia. After time spent with the NFL's Rams and Falcons, Goldberg entered the world of professional wrestling. Goldberg disposes of opponents in lightening fast fashion with one of his two famous finishing moves—The Spear (a running tackle) and The Jackhammer. Like Austin, Goldberg oozes individuality and an "I play by my rules" bravado.

The ECW

Extreme Championship Wrestling's weekly one hour broadcast kicks off with a shot of the organization's logo. Appropriately, the logo is wrapped in barbed wire. Playing to smaller crowds both live and on television, the ECW brand of wrestling is just what its name says—extreme. The ring skirting is emblazoned with the words "Blood and Guts." This is wrestling that's much more violent than the WWF and WCW brands. There are no pads or mats on the floor outside the ring to cushion dives and falls. The moves are more intense and dangerous. The crowd loves it as the wrestlers appear to literally beat each other. While the action is scripted, this stuff really looks like it hurts. The wrestlers use cinder blocks, blow torches, metal folding chairs, 8-foot tables, and barbed wire as weapons. There's lots of blood. The audience seems angry and I saw several giving the finger as the camera panned the crowd. The fans are so into it that they count outloud as one opponent beats another with consecutive punches to the face. One reviewer calls ECW "slamming action and cockfight-like atmosphere." During televised events, the ECW disallows profanity and male vs. female violence. The one-hour I viewed was all about hard-core wrestling with little off-stage melodrama. For the angry and crazed wrestling fanatic, the ECW is a place to let off steam.

What's the draw?

What is it about professional wrestling that's revived its popularity in today's culture and grown an enthusiastic audience that includes children of all ages?

First, there's no denying the fact that today's professional wrestling is entertaining. One fan expressed her love for the sport in a letter to *Entertainment Weekly* magazine: "HALLELUJAH!!! It's about time somebody recognized wrestling fans. As a 24-year-old college-educated woman, I'm proud to say I love this stuff. I look forward to the shenanigans of the fabulous-looking men each week. It has all the elements of a great television program: drama, heartbreak, romance, excitement, and intrigue! Not to mention really buff men in tight wrestling shorts!" Every wrestling broadcast I viewed was filled with non-stop action, lots of attitude, sensory overload, and the hook of ongoing melodramatic story lines. With each broadcast ending on a cliff-hanger, loyal viewers will definitely be back for more. At the same time, relatively new viewers will be tempted to take the bait and come back as well. Just like my grandmother and her soaps, today's viewers can't miss their "story." The combination of music, pyrotechnics, and multiple-camera angles combine to make wrestling a sport for the music video crowd.

Second, the acting and athleticism are fairly good. The fact that wrestling is known to be "sports entertainment" starring a cast of extreme characters wrapped up in an ongoing series of bizarre tales and relationships makes the ridiculousness of wrestling's over-acting actually serve as a draw. In the wrestling world, over-acting is good acting. And the sillier, the better. In addition, these folks perform amazing athletic stunts at the risk of doing great harm to their bodies. To wrestle professionally and survive, one must be fit, muscular, and agile. Today's behemoth wrestlers are not only actors, but gymnasts, acrobats, and ballerinas all wrapped up in one package. The choreographed physical "dance" of a wrestling match is demanding. From what I saw, it's got to hurt. The "reality" of wrestling was realized in May 1999 when WWF superstar Owen Hart was killed during a 60-foot fall while being lowered by cable into the ring during a pay-per-view event. In September 1999, The Droz suffered a severe spinal cord injury during a match. His prognosis is uncertain.

> *The diversity of the characters markets the "sport" by enabling everyone to find someone who reflects their cares, concerns, experience, and aspirations.*

Third, professional wrestling is marketed heavily to children of all ages. The army of professional wrestling followers is huge, growing, and diverse. Wrestling's appeal crosses into all age and socio-economic groups. When Vince McMahon says his WWF target audience is 15–24 year-old males, don't believe it. A walk through your local discount store will prove otherwise. Anything that can be stamped with a professional wrestling logo or photo is. From the television, to school halls, to store aisles, to the streets—professional wrestling's presence on merchandise is inescapable. Walk those same halls that our impressionable young elementary kids walk on a daily basis. Chances are you'll see the faces, logos, and sayings of today's wrestling stars. For our younger kids, wrestling's grabbed them like the yo-yos, hula hoops, and Ninja Turtles of years past. Wrestling has been marketed successfully to all ages. In today's culture, wrestling is "cool."

Fourth, wrestling serves as a vent for our culture's collective anger. Today's emerging generations are marked by brokenness. Usually, it starts with brokenness in the home. Too many are alienated from self, others, and God. One symptom is the growing undercurrent of anger that finds its expression in fits of anger carried out on playgrounds, on film, in music . . . and in the wrestling ring. Judging from the screaming legions in a wrestling audience who pump their fists and raise their middle fingers, wrestling is a steam-valve for their own anger. By living vicariously through the rage-filled relationships played out on wrestling's stage, the fans find expression for their anger. My guess is the wrestling subculture will only get more angry, demanding the edge of wrestling misbehavior be stretched even further. For years, we've heard angry kids describe how listening to rock's thundering riffs and throat-wrenching vocals is a temporary fix for dealing with rage. Wrestling is uniquely poised to fill that role as well.

Fifth, the diverse cast of characters offers every kid someone with whom to identify. Every wrestling fan has got a favorite—someone who is worthy of their applause and adoration. Kids angry at the world might be drawn to the brash individualism of Stone Cold Steve Austin or Goldberg. Girls who have been taken advantage of might be attracted to the muscular Chyna as she enters the ring to put men in their place. The quiet introvert might find a comrade in Mick Foley's character Mankind. Young males with a tendency to objectify women may like Jeff Jarrett or The Godfather. Kids with an interest in the occult might name Kane, The Undertaker, Sting, or the Acolytes as favorites. In the world of wrestling, the diversity of the characters markets the "sport" by enabling everyone to find someone who reflects their cares, concerns, experience, and aspirations.

Sixth, professional wrestling is a sport uniquely suited for our postmodern times. The emerging world view of postmodernism celebrates diversity and pluralism. The postmodern person inhabits a world where right and wrong no longer exist. Consequently, who's to say how "the game" of life is supposed to be played? Everyone becomes a god to themselves, making and changing the rules as they go along depending on how they feel at any given moment in time. Authority is to be rejected. All these elements of the postmodern world are evidenced and celebrated in the world of wrestling. The referees are there, but they have little or no control. There is no delineation between good and evil. With the disappearance of the babyface and heel, anything and everything decadent is celebrated with cheers and applause. How can a world that is increasingly moving away from rules, borders, and boundaries continue to get excited about rule-driven conventional sports like baseball and football? Instead, it's a guy like Stone Cold Steve Austin who's the consumate postmodern hero. Why? Because every one of his decisions and actions is justified by his credo, "Because Stone Cold said so!"

And seventh, the world of wrestling offers disconnected kids "a religious experience." The wrestlers are the gods. The merchandise serve as icons. The matches and events are "church." In a day and age where the church, for a variety of reasons, is being eliminated from the menu of youthful spiritual possibilities, wrestling is an attractive option. By sharing an interest in wrestling with others their age, kids have found a common experience to talk about. Their "fellowship" is built around wrestling.

How should parents respond?

What then, should concerned parents and youth workers make of today's world of wrestling? Can we use wrestling to gain a window into the world of today's youth? If so, what can we learn? And how should we respond to the confusing and unhealthy messages of wrestling? The Center for Parent/Youth Understanding (CPYU) offers the following analysis and suggestions:

First, realize that the world of professional wrestling offers us a window into the world of our kids and their culture. It's a mistake to shake our heads in disgust, walk away, and forfeit the opportunity to learn about our kids through their fascination with this fast-growing phenomenon. Wrestling is popular for numerous reasons. Our job is to discover what our kids see as the attraction. Begin by taking a look at the world of wrestling to gain a first-hand knowledge of what's out there. Then, sit down and discuss that world with your kids. If wrestling has become an obsession for your child you need to discover the reasons why. Does wrestling reflect what's going on in your child's heart? Does wrestling and its characters speak to their situation, hurts, or perceived lot in life? Is their involvement purely for entertainment or is it something more? If so, are there problems that need to be addressed?

Our support through boosting ratings and revenues sends a loud message to the wrestling world that they're giving us what we want.

Second, if your child is getting wrapped up in wrestling's anger and violence, something needs to be done. Work to discover the root cause of your child's attraction to wrestling anger. Dig deep to uncover reasons for their violent expressions of the same. Sometimes anger is justifiable. But inappropriate expressions of anger should be addressed immediately. Wrestlers model an approach to conflict resolution that's anything but positive—if someone is crossed, they beat the other person senseless and silly. Wrestling promotes no-holds barred violence. We must offer and model alternative outlets and responses to stem the growing tide of vengeance and violence in today's youth culture. We must teach our kids Biblical models of conflict resolution.

Third, we must actively undo wrestling's negative example and lessons about life. Some will laugh at the notion that wrestling is a powerful teacher—after all, "it's only entertainment!" Sure it's fake, but that doesn't negate the fact that wrestling can and does serve as a powerful teacher. Young children who are cognitively unable to separate fiction from reality don't know the difference. Ask any playground monitor about professional wrestling and they'll tell you stories of squelching recess tussles, both fake and real, that look a lot like pro wrestling matches. Wrestling *does* teach and influence young lives. Howard Spivak, chairman of the American Academy of Pediatrics task force on violence says, "These shows are extremely inappropriate models for children." Televised violence is linked to an increase in aggression among children. "A 1994 Israeli study of third through sixth graders showed that after the WWF started airing in Israel in the early 1990s, violent behavior—in the form of mock wrestling matches that often escalated to fighting and injuries—increased 'to a degree never known before.' When WWF airtime was cut back, the violence among school children diminished 'sharply.'" (*U.S. News & World Report*, 5/17/99). On a visit to our local K-Mart, I scanned the aisles of wrestling action figures and toys. There were many of all types. One action figure of The Rock came complete with a crate (for stuffing opponents in), a snow-shovel (for hitting opponents over the head), and a "head-dunkin' toilet." The box read, "ages 4 and up." Not surprisingly,

I've seen lots of kids imitate D-Generation X by yelling "SUCK IT!" while imitating X-Pac's chops to the groin.

Fourth, older children and adults should be challenged to consider wrestling's effect on them. While wrestling may not have the same directive power over adults as over young children, there is still an element of "teaching" involved. First, continued viewing desensitizes viewers, leading to relaxed standards of right and wrong. If we laugh or cheer for it, our guard is let down. Second, younger kids don't miss learning from our example. If we watch it, it's okay for them. If we laugh and cheer at it, we've given them permission to do the same.

Fifth, involvement indicates support. Our support through boosting ratings and revenues sends a loud message to the wrestling world that they're giving us what we want. In effect, we're telling them to "keep it up!"

Sixth, the amoral messages of wrestling should be aggressively countered with the truth. Postmodernity issues serious challenges to the standards of right and wrong that keep a culture in check. Wrestling's expressions of and contribution to this decline are seen in its lack of civility, disappearance of right and wrong, the rise of individual license, anti-authoritarianism, the decline of respect, the objectification of women, free use of profanity, fascination with depravity and darkness, and the elimination of personal responsibility. God's order demands a different view of life. Wrestling serves as a wake-up call for diligent parenting and ministry to kids. We must live out and communicate God's order and design for all of life.

Seventh, schools should not be an "arena" for professional wrestling. Of course, wise parents will disallow the T-shirts, toys, and other wrestling paraphernalia. The message of "Austin 3:16" is inappropriate—especially on a child's T-shirt. Where parents don't willingly exercise their responsibility, the local schools should enact dress-code standards which disallow such indecency and discourage wrestling behavior.

And finally, each of us should shift gears to invest our "professional wrestling time" more wisely. Parents of younger children should make that decision for them. Offer entertainment alternatives that are safe, healthy, and enjoyable. Parents of older children and teens might want to watch and discuss a match with their kids. Point out the negative aspects of wrestling while encouraging those children to invest in more wholesome viewing. If your relationship with your teen is marked by mutual respect, a "no-wrestling" directive will sit more easily.

I'll admit it—my week in wrestling left me facing a great dilemma. On the one side, I experienced first-hand the magnetic draw that this action-packed world has on kids. I understand why so many get hooked. But on the other hand, I felt like my morals and standards were body-slammed down to the mat. I was left with two conclusions: First, it's not a good thing so many individuals *and* our culture are hopping on board the pro wrestling bandwagon and climbing into the ring. And second, my mom the peace-maker was probably right!

7

Professional Wrestling Teaches Children Unsportsmanlike Values

Jim Waxmonsky and Eugene V. Beresin

Jim Waxmonsky is a resident in the McLean/Massachusetts General Hospital Child and Adolescent Psychiatry Program and a clinical fellow in psychiatry at Harvard Medical School. Eugene V. Beresin is the director of the Child and Adolescent Psychiatry Residency Training Program for Massachusetts General Hospital/McLean Hospital and an associate professor of psychiatry at Harvard Medical School.

Professional wrestling is often criticized for exposing children to excessive violence, sexual imagery, and profanity. However, a more serious threat lies in the potential for children to mistakenly perceive pro wrestling to be sport rather than entertainment. Most sports are healthy activities that instill positive values in children. However, wrestling is not sport—it could even be dubbed the "Anti-Sport" because it reinforces values diametrically opposed to those considered sportsmanlike. While only very young children are likely to act out the aggressive behavior they witness on wrestling shows, wrestling teaches older children that cheating and verbal intimidation are necessary to achieve success in life. Parents must explain the differences between sport and wrestling and encourage their children to participate in activities that teach good sportsmanship.

There is no denying that professional wrestling (PW) is firmly entrenched as part of modern culture. In 1999, the most-watched cable television show was the World Wrestling Federation (WWF)'s *WWF Raw,* which was more popular than *Monday Night Football* with teenage boys.[1] The WWF show, *Smackdown,* was the second-highest-rated network TV show.[2] PW is now shown in 120 countries, in 11 different languages.[1]

It also is evident that many children, both boys and girls, are drawn to wrestling. Fifteen percent of PW viewers are under the age of 11.[1] Children buy PW toys, watch their shows, practice their holds, and idealize their values. Although there is no denying PW's popularity, there is still great debate surrounding its impact. Specifically, many parents, teachers, and clinicians are concerned about the message that PW sends to children. PW has been criticized for its sex, violence, profanity, and advertising to children. Even such bastions of cultural morality as *Inside Edition* have hurled stones of criticism at PW.[1] In fact, criticizing wrestling has become such a pervasive social trend that PW has incorporated it into its own plots. The WWF has created a character called The Censor, Steven Richards. The Censor and his followers try to "censor" (which is a WWF euphemism for beat up) other wrestlers that they find objectionable.

Is pro wrestling a sport?

Television has certainly produced shows that are equally if not more violent and sexualized than PW. The problem with PW, which is also one of its greatest assets, is that it is a novel hybrid between sport and entertainment. In fact, wrestling promoters now prefer the designation "Sports Entertainment." American society has never really been exposed to such a combination before and is struggling with how to understand it. Is PW just another aggressive "extreme" sport, such as rugby or arena football, or is it more akin to a soap opera that features muscular men in combat instead of hideously wealthy socialites? The answer to this question will help determine what the potential impact of PW will be on children. The goal of this article is not to condemn PW, as it is clearly going to be a part of American culture for years to come. Rather, the goal is to analyze PW's broad appeal and predict the possible effects it will have on children who are exposed to significant amounts of it.

If we label [professional wrestling] a sport, it automatically gains credibility and acceptance whether it deserves it or not.

Wrestling, as sport, is probably one of the oldest athletic competitions in history and has a very rich heritage dating back before Ancient Rome. It is well established that amateur, or Greco-Roman, wrestling is a sport, but what about PW? Is it a sport or not? The answer to this question is critically important in determining how society perceives PW. The label of "sport" generally connotes a healthy activity that would probably be good for children. Although there is some debate about the value of specific sports such as hunting or boxing, society readily exposes children to many aggressive sports under the assumption that it will teach them useful competitive values. Sports are viewed as a wholesome arena where kids can learn values free of the anxieties of the adult world. Most adults would acknowledge that exposing children to sports is a part of good parenting, and there is substantial basis for this belief in the academic and popular literature. For example, a study by Pate and associates that surveyed over 14,000 teens observed that sports participation was associated with several positive behaviors. More specifically, both male and female teens who participated in sports were less likely to use cigarettes or other substances of abuse than teens who did not participate in sports. Female athletes had lower rates of sexual intercourse than those who did not play sports, and male athletes had lower rates of suicidal thoughts than their counterparts who did not participate in a sport.[3] The danger is that the word sport has a very precise connotation to it of being good for kids. If we label PW a sport, it automatically gains credibility and acceptance whether it deserves it or not, and it becomes hard to preach the evils of PW when we readily accept the violence in other sports.

To decide whether PW is a sport, we must first define the criteria for being a sport. Sports history expert Allen Guttmann has defined sport as a "form of play that is governed by rules and takes the form of a contest with a certain degree of physical activity."[4] Amateur wrestling clearly meets these criteria. PW is certainly a physical activity, but so are many actions that are not classified as sports. However, PW lacks rules and a sense of contest. PW certainly mimics these two aspects, just as soap operas mimic real relationships, but scripts and audience response drive PW, not rules, luck, or athletic prowess. The government has even attempted to determine whether PW is a sport. When PW became increasingly popular in the 1980s, New Jersey and several other states attempted to tax and legislate PW just as they would any other sport. The promoters of PW suddenly started using the phrase "sports entertainment" to describe PW. The New Jersey State legislature formally defined wrestling as "a bona fide athletic contest in which the participants struggle hand-to-hand with the object of winning . . . and in which any purpose of entertainment is secondary."[5] In contrast, the New Jersey legislature defined PW "as an activity in which participants struggle for the primary purpose of providing entertainment to spectators, rather than conducting a bona fide athletic contest."[5] Jim Steele, a sports sociologist, has even gone as far to say, "PW enables us to see what is not a sport in order that we have a better understanding of what a true sport is."[4] Clearly, PW is philosophically and legally not a sport. This leads to the question of what exactly PW is. What does the phrase "sports entertainment" mean? To answer this question intelligently, it is necessary to understand the origins of PW.

It is the "antisportiness" of [professional wrestling]
that presents the greatest danger to children, not the
vulgarity, violence, or nudity.

Professional wrestling dates back to the 1920s carnival circuits, where wrestlers would perform in front of local audiences. However, these matches did not draw well, as they were lengthy endurance battles devoid of fast-paced action. Consequently, the crowds dwindled. A group of vaudeville promoters saw potential in wrestling and began to host scripted matches with more action and flashier wrestlers. These matches were "fixed." There was a predetermined winner, with the wrestlers loosely following a script that consisted of dramatic physical feats that inflicted little real damage. Quickly, the crowds grew, and this is precisely the point when PW was born and left the arena of sports for the arena of entertainment. Over time, PW became more organized, more action-packed, and more dramatic—that is, more like fiction and less like sports. Now it is the scripts, the characters, and the drama that people tune in for, rather than the athletics. The sole purpose of PW matches is to engage the audience so that they will continue to watch. Every move and word is carefully crafted to evoke a strong emotional response, whether love or hatred, that will keep the audience fixated. In this sense, PW has evolved into a piece of fiction that rivals the latest Steven Spielberg movie or the newest television drama.

The fact that PW is entertainment does not make it inherently a subject for public concern. PW promoters have been quite open about the fact that the outcome of the matches is predetermined (of course their revelation was politely prompted by risk of possible legal repercussions). Nobody is really fooled into being a PW fan; most fans, from grade-school up, know that the winner is predetermined and that the physical combat is at least partially embellished. The fact that the debunking of PW has not diminished its appeal is really not surprising, once we realize that PW's appeal is due largely to its stories, and not its pseudo-athletics. It is hardly even defined in athletic terms anymore. One *TV Guide* summary for a PW show described a love triangle between wrestlers, while another character was the victim of a vehicular hit-and-run. There was no mention of anything remotely suggesting an athletic event; therefore, unless we knew this was a PW show, we would have sworn we were reading about a soap opera.

What is really so bad about PW? Is it not just another television show that grabs ratings through sex and violence? Clearly, it is that, but it is also something more. PW is different from soap operas, video games, or horror movies because PW closely resembles sports, and, despite the effort of the New Jersey legislature and a handful of academics, the public—including parents and children—largely views PW as a sport. Even educated health professionals have fallen into the trap. A study featured in the American Academy of Pediatrics (AAP) newsletter looking at the effects of television violence on children did not include PW shows. The researchers included comedies, movies, dramas, music videos, and cartoons, but excluded sports, news, and "entertainment sports programs." The study did not label PW as a sport, but it did categorize it with such entities as baseball and golf and separated it from other fictional shows.[6]

The "Anti-Sport"

The danger in categorizing PW as a sport, other than offending sports sociologists and possibly the New Jersey legislature, is that the powerful connotations associated with the word sport will be applied to PW. As noted above, for many parents, "sports" is akin to saying, "kid-tested and approved." PW is not a sport, so it should not get this benefit. It is the id run wild, a virtual overflow of primary-process [primitive-level thinking], where sex and violence rules and where steel chairs are the most effective problem-solving device. It teaches the exact opposite message of sports and is, in many aspects, the antithesis of sport, or "The Anti-Sport." However, children and adolescents will be likely to view it as sport because it looks like other sports, and consequently they may then apply PW's values for conflict resolution to other sports as well as other aspects of life. This may be particularly true for younger children, who do not have the cognitive capacity to understand the highly dramatic, fictional underpinnings of PW.

For adults, this concern may not be a significant issue, because they can appreciate that PW is really fictional violence, and not sport. However, children are immersed in sports in our culture from a very early age. There is an expectation that children will learn, from sports, rules for managing aggression and how to compete in a controlled fashion. This is a reasonable expectation, because in sports there are rules that serve as boundaries for aggression and rules that ensure the champion is the entity most deserving of victory. It is hard to find any other aspect of life where criteria for victory are so clearly defined and rigidly adhered to by all participants. Certainly, such criteria do not exist for relationships, careers, or—dare one say it—presidential elections.

Sporting events are essentially controlled conflicts between two entities, whether they are schools, cities, or nations. Such conflicts could not safely occur in other realms. The referees and commissioners are there to strictly enforce the rules and are normally granted an almost religious respect by the athletes. To quote the old baseball adage, "There is no winning an argument with the umpire." Henricks described each sporting event as a series of "critical moments," such as "the bases loaded with a full count" or "fourth down and one," which are mediated by the unifying force of the referee.[7] A repeating cycle of opposition and unification is played out on the athletic field just as Sigmund Freud described the interplay of intrapsychic conflicts. The battle is then decisively resolved, and a champion is crowned who will reign until the next season. The athletes have no recourse but to accept the champion, as they are bound by the rules. The event typically ends with a show of friendship between the two players/teams. Once the game has ended, so too does the aggression between the athletes. Any aggression outside of the playing field is quickly stopped and severely punished by the governing authority.

If the rules of sport are removed, what is left is uncontrolled primal aggression, where the most violent and persistent attain triumphs. This is precisely the case of PW, "The Anti-Sport."

It is the "antisportiness" of PW that presents the greatest danger to children, not the vulgarity, violence, or nudity. To truly understand this, one needs an understanding of the psychology of PW and its value system.

The mythology

PW is basically a reincarnation of the classical morality plays of ancient Greek dramas. Henricks argues that the basic plot of a professional wrestling match posits physical force as the singular effective way for settling the dispute between good and evil.[7] These two opposing forces will meet in the ring, usually with some story surrounding their confrontation. The story lines often involve classic mythological themes, such as the son rebelling against the father, or the damsel, kidnapped by the villain, who now requires rescue.

Zengota[8] considers individual wrestlers more akin to comic book characters than to any type of athlete. They are shallow-but-familiar stereotypes that dress in garish costumes and perform superhuman feats of strength and endurance, often using special, almost magical submission holds. A good portion of the story line is developed to set up the wrestlers as immensely powerful heroes or villains that the audience can love or hate but could never emulate. The wrestlers have evolved into champions of good and evil. The hero abides by the rules (for a little while, at least) and upholds the honor of the people. He thrives on the cheers of the spectators, getting stronger as they yell louder. The villain is completely evil. He is the bully who preys on the weak and humiliates people at every turn, but who will typically run or resort to tricks when confronted with a real challenge. He taunts and degrades the audience, evoking loud rebuttals from the crowd.

[Professional wrestling] sends the message that deceit and cheating are the key to victories—not strength, speed, or intelligence.

Unlike most team sports, there are no hometown favorites in PW. The heroes are the same in New York as they are in Los Angeles. However, heroes can become villains, and vice versa. The conversions are immediate and dramatic. The hero-turned-villain is especially hated because he has abandoned the fans, whereas the villain-turned-hero is praised and admired because he has seen the error of his ways and converted. At the most primal level, the fans are actually rooting for the triumph of good or evil as much as they are rooting for an individual performer. They are rooting for the hero that they always wanted to be or the villain who acts out their hidden aggressive fantasies.

Besides being mythical, the wrestlers are immensely simplistic stereotypes of images from the current culture. The villains typically will hail from the country that is presently in conflict with the United States, such as Russia or some nation in the Middle East. When ethnic enemies run out, PW reverts to other stock-character types, such as the ghetto ruffian or the pretentious aristocrat. PW also makes use of racial and sexual stereotypes, such as the wild African savage or the effeminate homosexual. Because of the exaggerated and simplistic nature of the PW stereotypes, it is quite easy for children to deduce that the villain is the villain because he is from the Middle East or because he is from the ghetto, which can create dangerous associations in their naive minds.

The failure of traditional sporting values

PW maintains the pretense of sport. There are rules, referees, championship trophies, and commissioners in PW, but as Henricks[7] stated, PW is based on a "quite systematic transgression of norms and values." The villains will violate the rules from the beginning and either receive a verbal warning from the referee or their violation is simply ignored. A wrestler never gets disqualified for using an illegal tactic or refusing to break a hold. In fact, the success of the villain is directly correlated with his willingness to break the rules. Typically, the champion will abide by the rules and be constantly frustrated by the cheating of the villain. The hero usually only wins when he abandons the rules and resorts to villainous tactics. The rules are nothing more than a burden to the hero, an annoyance that needs to be discarded in order to win the match. This pretense of rules presents an even scarier message than if PW were to have no rules at all. In a free-for-all, one would expect the strongest or smartest to win, but in PW, the winner is the one who can most efficiently bend the rules to his advantage. PW sends the message that deceit and cheating are the key to victories—not strength, speed, or intelligence.

Likewise, PW has referees dressed in the standard garb of officials, black pants and a striped shirt. Referees in PW were originally added to pace the matches so that they did not run too long or end too quickly. The referees tend to be very small, older men who are dwarfed by the wrestlers. In modern times, they have also taken on the role of court jester. They are invariably ignored and are often mocked or even physically abused by the wrestlers, much to the delight of the fans. At times, the wrestlers themselves serve as referees, and they inevitably favor one wrestler over the other and openly help one side to win. In any sport, physical contact with the referees results in an immediate and severe penalty. In PW, it is a strategic and laudable maneuver to knock the referee unconscious. PW also has commissioners. In sports, commissioners are the ultimate authorities who are supposed to update the rules to keep the game fair and settle disputes between teams/athletes. In wrestling, however, the commissioners have become a part of the story line and have even wrestled, themselves. They hold grudges against wrestlers and often break or blatantly change the rules to guarantee that their favorites have an advantage. In the WWF, various members of the McMahon family, who are the real-life founders of the WWF, serve as the commissioner and governing body. However, the McMahons have come to resemble the Ewing family of "Dallas" fame. They are as villainous as the wrestlers and certainly do not act as keepers of the peace.

Somebody has to be humiliated, whether it is by being beaten into psuedounconsciousness or by some other incredibly humiliating act.

PW also has championships and title belts, but controversy surrounds every victory. As all great works of literature have shown, good or evil never completely triumphs, but rather there is a perpetual series of battles between these two powerful forces. The same happens in PW—there is never a clear victor; instead, there is a series of rematches and disputed victories that would make even a professional boxing promoter envious. There is always some controversy surrounding the champion's victory that will force him to fight again. Often, it is unclear who exactly is the "winner," as the person who won the match will get beaten senseless by his opponent after the match has ended. Since the wrestlers have become such grand icons of good and evil, a simple 1-2-3 pinfall would not be an adequate resolution for the crowd. As Zengota described, a clash of such gigantic forces must have a climactic ending; therefore, the one requirement is that somebody has to be humiliated, whether it is by being beaten into pseudounconsciousness or by some other incredibly humiliating act.[8] Such acts have included having trash strewn on the loser, spray-painting him, or even simulating oral sex over the loser's hapless body.

The other main tenet of wrestling is that verbal intimidation leads to success. The wrestlers who win are the ones who evoke the loudest crowd response, whether it is positive or negative. Therefore the rudest, loudest, and cruelest villains float to the top because they evoke the most anger from the fans and keep them watching on a regular basis. This connection nicely demonstrates for children that verbal intimidation and bullying will lead to success and that these tactics are a very effective way to get one's needs met. Hence, the main concern should not simply be that children are reciting vulgar phrases that they learned on PW but that they might actually think that telling somebody to "suck it" or spraying them with beer will help them to achieve their aspirations and gain the admiration of their peers.

In summary, PW is The Anti-Sport because traditional sporting values lead to predictable failure in PW, whereas the systematic cheating that leads to success in PW would result in a lifetime ban in any other sport. PW's message is just as compelling for children who know that PW is "embellished." For most school-age children and older, the greatest danger of PW is not that they will slam their friends through the kitchen table—because most children know that an oak dining room table will not break in half like those on TV. The greatest danger is that they will deduce that verbal intimidation and cheating are a successful combination for negotiating life's challenges. For children who have difficulty distinguishing fantasy from reality, the dangers of PW are much more concrete. Children below the age of seven or older children with developmental delays are more likely to directly mimic the wrestling moves they see on TV, because they do not have the cognitive capacity to deduce that the outcomes will be much more serious in real life. So what should parents do when their children want to watch endless hours of PW? Many parents have banned their kids from watching any PW, ignoring the fact that children can easily access PW outside of their homes. Some parents try to solve the PW dilemma by telling their children that it is fake, thinking they have ruined the appeal of PW for their kids. Unfortunately, that is like telling kids there is no Santa Claus and then expecting them not to want presents on Christmas. Just as most kids know Santa is mythical, they know that PW violence is simulated. However, this revelation does not diminish their interest in it, nor does it make them less susceptible to the messages of PW. Other parents have become completely exasperated, concluding there is no way to protect their children from the onslaught of PW—and wait in fear for their children to become the next generation of professional wrestlers.

Protecting the children

Even though parents cannot effectively shelter their children from PW, they do have significant power when it comes to shaping the impact of PW on their children. Parents need to be realistic and accept the fact that their kids are drawn to PW, as it has many attractive features, such as comic book–like characters, lots of action, and suspenseful plots that evolve in a dramatic fashion. The parents' role should be to teach their children that PW is The Anti-Sport, because children will not be able to make this distinction on their own.

First, even if parents are fans of PW, they need to realize that it will not teach their kids anything useful about good sportsmanship or about controlling aggression. If parents choose to watch PW, they should do so on their own time; children will interpret their parents' interest as a sign that it is okay for them to watch PW.

Second, without being overly critical, parents need to combat PW's message of intimidation and rule-breaking. To do this, they need to sit with their children and watch these shows and explain to them that PW is entertainment, just like a movie or Saturday morning cartoons. They need to identify the differences between sports and PW. Most importantly, parents need to emphasize that successful tactics in PW are unacceptable, unproductive, and often illegal in any real-world venue, whether it is the athletic field or the schoolyard.

Children should be encouraged to develop other interests if they are almost solely devoted to PW. However, parents need to be realistic and not try to substitute piano lessons or the math club for PW. A child who is drawn to PW might enjoy participating in a legitimate sport or another stimulating activity that is rule-based and does not have PW's anti-sport message. The martial arts, for example, are excellent alternatives, since they embrace control, self-defense, discipline, and respect. To be successful, the transition needs to be gradual and subtle. Parental attempts at forcing children into activities are rarely successful; instead, parents should expose children to a variety of activities and let them select the ones they like the most.

Parents need to emphasize that successful tactics in [professional wrestling] are unacceptable, unproductive, and often illegal in any real-world venue.

Parents also need to recognize that there are many factors that will influence the effect of PW on their children. Parents should monitor all of the TV programs their children watch and not just PW shows, paying special attention to those with violent or other adult themes. The methods used within the family for resolving conflict are critically important determinants of how children will handle their own conflicts. Any child who repeatedly witnesses aggressive physical or verbal confrontations between his or her caretakers is more likely to engage in such acts. Rules at home should be fair, clearly explained, and executed as consistently as possible. Also, parents should be aware that children with difficult temperaments and those with impulsive, externalizing [acting out] behavior disorders are likely to be more susceptible to the effects of PW. Children who participate in legitimate sports may be more adept at distinguishing the difference between PW and sports.

The entertainment industry also has a role to play. It needs to recognize the potentially deleterious effects of PW on children and stop aggressively marketing PW shows and merchandise to them. PW shows should be targeted only to mature audiences and not be included in Saturday morning television schedules. Likewise, PW merchandise should not include action figures or others toys designed for young children. The conclusions reached in this article should not lead to banning PW from television; there are many other offensive TV shows that would be better gone from television before PW.

By itself, PW will not increase the prevalence of conduct [i.e., behavioral] or antisocial personality disorders. Adults, for the most part, have the capacity to recognize that the tactics and values of PW are not acceptable in the real world. They can safely watch PW for what it is, entertainment, albeit violent. PW's impact on children, however, may be quite different. Children do not have the luxury of being fully able to make the distinction between reality and fantasy, and may not be able to separate the "rules" of PW from the norms of daily life. Hence, the entertainment industry needs to take this into account when considering the broadcasting of PW. The standards for children need to be different from those for adults.

This author (JW) feels compelled to end by saying that I enjoy PW and have been known to watch a few minutes now and then, even outside of research purposes. However, sometimes I think that I may have to cut back, as my wife says I am becoming a little too aggressive when playing Scrabble. I guess she does not find it amusing when I yell, "Do you smell what The Rock is cooking?" whenever I get a triple word score.

References

1. Rosellini L: Lords of the Ring. *U.S. News & World Report,* May 17, 1999, p. 52.

2. Meltz B: Wrestling with WWF. *Boston Globe,* Jan. 20, 2000, pp. E1, E4.

3. Pate E, Trost S, Levin S, et al: Sports participation and health-related behaviors among U.S. youth. *Arch Pediatr Adolesc Med* 2000; 154:904–911.

4. Farrey T: Wrestle with This [25 paragraphs]. Pro Wrestling's Grip on America [online series], 4, April 2, 1999. Available at: http://espn.go.com/otl/wrestling/day3_part1.html [5/17/2000].

5. McCallum J, O'Brien R: Scorecard: Pro Wrestling Is Fake. *Sports Illustrated,* March 23, 1997, p. 23.

6. Shifrin D: Three-Year Study Documents Nature of Television Violence. *AAP News,* August 1998 (from http://www.aap.org/advocacy/shifrin898.htm).

7. Henricks T: Professional wrestling as moral order. *Sociological Inquiry* 1974; 44: 177–188.

8. Zengota E: Versus: Archetypal Images in Professional Wrestling. *Quadrant* 1991; 24:27–39.

8

Backyard Wrestling Is Growing in Popularity

Daniel B. Wood

Daniel B. Wood is a staff writer for the Christian Science Monitor, *a national daily newspaper. He covers a variety of issues, including subjects of interest to young people such as education and entertainment.*

Teenagers from working-class neighborhoods have joined an estimated 1,000 backyard wrestling federations in which they emulate their professional wrestling idols, sometimes emerging from the matches covered in blood. Despite the risk of serious injury, backyard wrestlers perform perilous stunts with little supervision and no regulation. Some organizations do have the help of professional trainers, but both the World Wrestling Federation and World Championship Wrestling discourage these backyard leagues. Backyard wrestlers who hope to become pros face poor if not impossible odds: the pro leagues recruit professional and collegiate athletes, and of these, few make it to the pro ranks.

O n Saturdays from 3 P.M. to sundown, the backyards of this working-class neighborhood echo with the sound of body slams.

- Terry Adams, 16, who goes by the nickname "Twisted," launches a "Vader bomb"—a horizontal dive from the third ring rope, landing on his opponent's neck.
- Dirrick Fretz, 18, polishes his "moonsault," a back flip off the corner ring post onto the stomach of an adversary lying below.
- Justin Sullivan, 15, takes direct whacks to the forehead from an opponent swinging a metal folding chair. Later, the chair is covered in barbed wire. At the end of the match, Justin proudly wipes away the blood streaming down his face.

Along with some 50 other aspirants, these teens gather each weekend to wrestle, inventing ever more extreme moves, which they hope will open doors to a future on TV or in front of paying crowds.

This "backyard federation" is one of an estimated 1,000 nationwide that have emerged in the past two years. It's become one of the most seductive new outlets for teenage boys seeking both thrills and a future in big-time wrestling.

But the trend is raising serious safety concerns amid larger questions over escalating violence in society and sport.

To these weekend warriors, the matches offer a combination of savage fun and an outlet for aggression. Many harbor hopes of one day being discovered by talent scouts for the World Wrestling Federation (WWF) or World Championship Wrestling (WCW). The WWF's programming is seen by some 20 million viewers weekly, many of whom are teenage boys, drawn in by the extravaganzas of soap-opera story lines, comic-book characters, and over-the-top stunts that now regularly include flips off arena balconies.

Because these backyard federations are unregulated and largely unsupervised, serious injuries are a common phenomenon.

Yet because these backyard federations are unregulated and largely unsupervised, serious injuries are a common phenomenon, as the teens try to emulate their TV idols. On this particular day, a half dozen boys leave the ring covered in their own blood.

"We now have a group of post-pubescent youth coming through the most vulnerable stage of masculinity, bombarded by TV images they feel they ought to be able to emulate," says Alan Klein, a sports psychologist at Northeastern University, in Boston. "Some try to copy [professional wrestling moves] as a proving ground; for others it's a way to gain acceptance; for still others, it's just pure acting out."

The top two leagues these teens aspire to, the WWF and WCW, openly discourage backyard federations. And a growing chorus of parents, communities, and schools is calling for a stop to the activity, even as law enforcement largely looks the other way.

"We are adamantly opposed to the concept of 'backyard wrestling,'" says Bruce Prichard, vice president of talent relations for the WWF. "Any attempt by our fans to emulate our superstars' physicality is extremely dangerous and irresponsible. Backyard wrestling is not a path to WWF superstardom, and we accept no applications or videotapes from those who practice it."

Wrestling wannabes

Those comments, and the scarcity of professional league contracts—there are fewer than 250 at the moment, leagues say—are in no way a deterrent to these wrestling wannabes.

"This has been my dream as long as I can remember," says Danny Rivera, a 15-year-old Latino who has been practicing for eight months and wrestles under the moniker "Stray Cat." He points to his forehead, arms, and torso, where scars have been left by thumbtacks, light bulbs, barbed wire, and even fire used in practice performances.

He displays a wide leather championship belt made of a rotary saw blade painted gold and embossed with the title, "Youth Suicide Hard-core Champion."

"I got a reputation for being hard-core right away," says Danny.

Andy "Hair" Johnson, 16, began practicing punches and leg drops on a family mattress five years ago. He wrestles and runs track at his high school, but enjoys this much more.

"This is just pure, out and out fun," says Andy. "This is like my total dream to go pro. People say it's dangerous but that's why we're here practicing, 'cause if someone got really hurt that wouldn't be any fun."

With similar single-mindedness, Andy's colleagues spend the afternoon practicing basic moves known as arm drags, hip tosses, leg drags, and drop kicks. They claim they are under the tutelage of two local trainers who have trained extensively in the pro leagues.

"You absolutely have to have serious training at this or you are going to hurt yourself," says one of these trainers, an 18-year-old named Leroy who asked that his last name not be used.

With a $2,400 loan from his grandparents, Leroy just finished a 12-month course with a local pro-wrestling school he says wishes to remain anonymous. "The big leagues don't like these backyard federations, but I'm here helping out because these guys are all my friends," he says.

"I get really angry when people just think we're a bunch of punks. We're out here practicing regularly just like pros."

The other trainer here, known simply as Andre, is an 18-year-old who has been wrestling since he was 12. Sidelined by a back injury after diving out onto a table covered with barbed wire and light bulbs, Andre recently purchased the group's professional-quality wrestling ring for $5,000.

Until this week, the group had been practicing on wood planks suspended on stacks of old tires. The 50 or so teens are now pooling their resources to start their own league, rent an arena, and charge admission.

Selling the act

As heavy metal music blares out of a dusty boombox, Andre barks out commands like a high school coach, as his friends run through choreographed moves in the ring.

Besides performing several routine maneuvers that include back flips, hairpulling, head locks, and body slams, each is asked to "sell" the act by grimacing in pain, holding body parts as if injured.

Onlookers chant for more as wrestlers whack the mat, wince, quiver, and shriek. As each boy exits the ring, he is asked how it went.

"A lot of people think wrestling is a fake sport, but we get hurt all the time," says Dirrick Fretz, who performs as "Trizzy Dee." "I get really angry when people just think we're a bunch of punks. We're out here practicing regularly just like pros."

The kids say they get encouragement from adults such as Pam Adams, whose backyard hosts the ring, and whose son participates regularly.

"I support the kids a lot," says Ms. Adams, an unemployed mother whose husband was killed in a truck crash one year ago. "People squeal that this is so dangerous, but you can get hurt in hockey and football just as bad. I would rather have these kids here where I can see them than out on the streets doing drugs."

Hidden dangers

But Andy Gillentine, who teaches the psychology of coaching at Mississippi State University says this kind of wrestling is dangerous, since participants don't use padding and are attempting stunts that are more dangerous than they know.

"These kids have an invincibility complex, like kids in all sports," says Dr. Gillentine, who has conducted three research studies for the WCW. "But they are mimicking moves that have taken years to perfect by seasoned pros."

Indeed, league spokesmen say the majority of wrestlers they put on contract are top professional and collegiate athletes. Case in point is current WWF champ, Kurt Angle. The best wrestler in the US during his college years, Angle went on to win the Olympic gold medal in 1996. When he entered the WWF, he still had to go through two years of training before the league felt he was ready to perform.

The WWF says it has 36 schools in four geographic areas of the US where aspirants can train. But they underline the fact that few ever make it to the pro ranks.

"When you realize there are only about 250 wrestlers on contract in the top three leagues, you realize your chances of hitting the big time are far less than an actor has of making it to Broadway, a football player to the NFL, or a basketball player to the NBA," says Alan Sharp, spokesman for the WCW.

Still, teenagers often think they are the exception. Many hope to be like Terry Funk, a WCW legend who still continues at age 56—though Mr. Funk wouldn't recommend following in his footsteps.

"I think we have too much violence in wrestling, on TV in general, and society as a whole," says Funk. "If I had a son, I would steer him away from wrestling. It was fun for me, but for most it's not healthy in the long run."

9

Professional Wrestling Is a Scapegoat for Society's Ills

Henry Frederick

Henry Frederick is a crime reporter with the News-Journal, *a Daytona Beach, Florida, newspaper. A professional wrestling fan, Frederick also writes a weekly wrestling column, "Wrestling ReWind," for the newspaper's online edition.*

Blaming professional wrestling for violence in the workplace and at schools is unfair. All professional sports involve violence. While the violence in professional sports is real, however, the violence in wrestling is scripted. Rather than use pro wrestling as a scapegoat for society's problems, parents should spend more time with their children. If their children are watching pro wrestling, parents need to explain that the matches are fake and should not be imitated.

I am college-educated, married with two children and own my own home.

Oh, and I am a wrestling fan.

A big fan, at that.

It seems fashionable these days to bash the world of professional wrestling. What with school shootings, violence in the work place and juvenile crime on the rise, what better scapegoat than wrestling.

Wrestling is simply a parody of society at large with larger-than-life musclemen and big-breasted women extolling the virtues of good and evil in our fast-paced society.

And "fast-paced" is the key here.

We as a society don't make the time for our children. It's much easier to sit them in front of a TV and have the Road Runner and the Coyote occupy their time. That is, if we're even home.

With America's economic prosperity at record highs, the pressure to bring home the bucks means less time for the kids. In many households, what was the nuclear family is vanishing quickly. Children today are more sophisticated because more is available to them, including cable television, the Internet and hand-held video games.

Parents need to take responsibility for what their children are watching and explain to them the significance of what's being shown. The violence on wrestling is scripted; that means it is fake. The violence in other sports is real—National Hockey League fights with sticks, brawls on the pitcher's mound and a 300-plus pound National Football League player pummeling an official for accidentally throwing a flag in his eye.

"There's violence in all sports today," notes Steve Ciacciarelli, editor of *Wrestling World* magazine. "Anyone who watches wrestling knows it's like watching a cartoon or the Three Stooges. People don't go walking around poking fingers in people's eyes like Larry, Mo and Curly do they? No, of course not."

Taking it for what it's worth

Most critics of wrestling never take the time to watch it so they don't appreciate what it's all about. It's a male soap opera intended for young men. The shows are labeled as "TV 14" and shown on cable outlets. The WWF in particular has the highest rated cable show, *WWF Raw is War* shown 9 P.M. Mondays on USA network. And wrestling toys outsell Pokemon.

Wrestlers have two books, The Rock with *The Rock Says*, and Mick Foley with *Mankind, Have a Nice Day!* at Nos. 1 and 4, respectively, on the *New York Times* Bestsellers List.

In fact, Foley's book topped the list in November 1999. Wrestling pay-per-views gross more than boxing championships and rock concerts.

As for Coca-Cola pulling out of WWF's *Smackdown* telecast because of perceived violence, the soda giant is based in Atlanta, home of the rival wrestling federation, World Championship Wrestling. Put two and two together.

Parents need to take responsibility for what their children are watching and explain to them the significance of what's being shown.

I like wrestling. My wife hates it. She thinks it's juvenile, which it is. For me, it's an escape from the daily pressures of life. My 6-year-old son, Little Henry, watches it with me. I explain to him that it's fake and shouldn't be copied. He responds, "I already know that, Dad."

My teen-age daughter, Joanna, identifies with wrestling as something to laugh with, as in The Rock with his inane sayings and "hot wrestling moves."

She's not going to school and pile-driving the teacher.

Parents who grew up on baseball and Little League are frustrated because their children are turning to wrestling. Parents need to do more than sign their children up for sports. They could brighten a child's face by playing catch in the yard once in a while.

"Big Sexy" Kevin Nash, a seasonal resident of Ponce Inlet and star in the WCW, says, "It's too easy to blame society's problems on wrestling. This is entertainment. It's fun. Most people take it for what it's worth."

As for emulating sports figures, children, especially teen-agers relate more to wrestlers because the likes of Seattle's Ken Griffey Jr. are more interested in seeking $100 million-plus contracts than signing autographs. These greedy ball players have forgotten their true fan base. And those who want to focus on wrestling need look no further than the esteemed NFL and its spate of homicides. Folks, that's real and far more damaging to our children.

10

Professional Wrestling Is a Form of Political Protest

Neal Gabler

Neal Gabler is a cultural historian and film critic who hosts the Public Broadcasting System review series Sneak Previews *and introduces programming on the cable television station American Movie Classics. Gabler is the author of* Life the Movie: How Entertainment Conquered Reality.

During 1999, more than 35 million Americans tuned in each week to watch professional wrestling on television. Pro wrestlers have become sought-after celebrities, and wrestler Jesse "The Body" Ventura was elected governor of Minnesota. One explanation for wrestling's popularity is that it provides disempowered Americans a way to express their anger and frustration. In the past, wrestlers were divided into good guys and bad guys. Today, wrestlers are almost entirely bad guys battling for power, money, or vengeance in an amoral universe, often forming shifting alliances in opposition to their corporate controllers. By identifying with these characters, fans are able to vicariously break society's moral strictures and express their rage against the forces that limit their lives.

In early 1999, while mainstream news outlets were preoccupied with the impeachment trial [of Bill Clinton] or the Kosovo bombing or the massacre at Columbine High School, millions of Americans were focused on another grim human drama. A satanic cult called the Ministry of Darkness, under the command of a tattooed behemoth named the Undertaker, who had an eerie habit of rolling his pupils under his eyelids and baring his teeth in a sickening smile, had forged what one commentator called an "unholy alliance" with the Corporation, a massive entertainment conglomerate headed by an arrogant, ambitious young entrepreneur named Shane McMahon.

McMahon seemed undeterred by the fact that the Undertaker had recently abducted his teenage sister Stephanie, strapped her to a cross, and demanded that she marry the evil one. Only a last-minute rescue by a grisly, shaved-pated hero named Stone Cold Steve Austin saved Stephanie from this horrible fate, though Austin was the sworn enemy of Stephanie's father, Vince McMahon, a power-mad industrialist who had headed the Corporation before being ousted by his own son and who had actually come to blows with Austin while trying to assert his authority over him.

If all this sounds like some kind of perverse soap opera, welcome to the new world of professional wrestling.

The success of wrestling

As virtually all America must know by now, during 1998 and 1999 wrestling has been enjoying one of its periodic upswings, though this one may top them all. Its promoters claim that 35 million Americans watch professional wrestling on television each week. And seven wrestling programs, led by the World Wrestling Federation's *Raw Is War* and the World Championship Wrestling's *Monday Nitro,* consistently rank among the 10 highest rated shows on cable television.

Reinforcing the ratings success story, a March 1999 edition of *TV Guide* with wrestling stars on the cover outsold the Oscar edition by 500,000 copies, and an issue of *Playboy* featuring a photo spread on the World Wrestling Federation women's champion, a buxom blond named Sable, sold more than one million copies on the newsstand. The magazine put Sable on the cover again in September 1999—making her the first woman since the 1950s to land two covers in a single year.

Hollywood is also taking notice. Superstar Goldberg was recruited for Jean-Claude Van Damme's *Universal Soldier: The Return,* and both Warner Bros. and Mandalay Pictures have wrestling movies in development. At the same time, the WWF's Vince McMahon bought Debbie Reynolds's bankrupt Las Vegas casino and plans to turn it into a wrestling-themed hotel, while McMahon's rival organization, the World Championship Wrestling, has opened a new theme restaurant in Vegas. All told, by one account wrestling grossed only $100,000 less than major-league baseball did in 1998.

Ventura promised to bodyslam social problems the way he had bodyslammed his opponents in the ring.

Ask why wrestling is enjoying this popularity explosion, and observers may point to the symbiosis between wrestling, which is relatively inexpensive to produce and infinitely recyclable, and cable television, which has thousands of hours to fill. Or they may point to the fact that wrestling has become vastly more sophisticated in its packaging and marketing, allowing it to tap new, more upscale audiences. Or they may simply say that pro wrestling is an American staple that has always enjoyed surges in popularity after fallow periods and that this is just another of those booms, like the one that occurred in the 1980s, during Hulk Hogan's Hulkamania.

All of these explanations are plausible enough. But the most dramatic certification of wrestling's new place in the public consciousness, the election in November 1998 of onetime wrestling bad guy Jesse "the Body" Ventura to the governorship of Minnesota may provide the real answer to wrestling's recent ascent. By embracing his wrestling persona rather than distancing himself from it, Ventura positioned himself as the renegade independent running against the discredited political "corporations" of Republicans and Democrats. Ventura promised to bodyslam social problems the way he had bodyslammed his opponents in the ring.

Most political analysts were appalled by the idea of a wrestler winning in the political arena, but now that former champion Bob Backlund is running for Congress from Connecticut, and Hulk Hogan is considering a run for the presidency, Minnesotans may simply have been ahead of the curve. What they seemed to recognize was that wrestling and politics are both ways to express anger and disaffection, and whatever else it signified, Ventura's election was a testament to how effectively wrestling had performed that task—for if the Body turned politics into a form of wrestling, he could do so only because wrestling had itself become a potent form of populist politics. Or put another way, where politics was failing, wrestling was succeeding.

Spectacle, not sport

Almost from the moment wrestling turned professional, late in the nineteenth century, it was tainted by suspicions that it was less a sport than a spectacle. As early as the 1920s, when Ed "Strangler" Lewis was the reigning champion and wrestling drew crowds that numbered in the tens of thousands, sophisticated fans were distinguishing between "shooting" matches that were supposedly on the level and "working" matches that weren't. In 1936, when internecine warfare between promoters triggered a widely publicized federal investigation of match fixing, the "sport" was further besmirched. Not until the late 1940s and the advent of television did it begin to recover.

When wrestling did resurface, it had reformed by purging itself of the sporting element altogether. In its place arose an ongoing political allegory staged as a theatrical spectacle. Now wrestling had its own set of rigid and immediately recognizable conventions. Combatants were divided, in wrestling parlance, into "heels" (bad guys) and "babyfaces" (good guys). Heels were dishonest. They would gouge or poke eyes, yank hair, choke, kick, punch, and deploy every other possible form of chicanery. Frequently, they were accompanied by a manager who distracted the referee so the heel could engage in more nefarious activity. Often the manager himself kicked and pummeled opponents who had fallen outside the ring.

This was, in effect, life pared to its essentials—a Manichaean world of the good and the bad, the honest and the corrupt, the skillful and the loutish. In his famous 1952 essay on wrestling, the French critic Roland Barthes remarked on the show's clarity, its "perfect intelligibility of reality," and compared it to the commedia dell'arte, in which characters "display in advance, in their costumes and attitudes, the future contents of their parts. . . ." Other social critics compared wrestling to Japanese Kabuki or the medieval morality play in its simplicity and rigidity. In an American context, it was, in the words of Sharon Mazer—a medieval scholar and the author of *Professional Wrestling: Sport and Spectacle*—a form that serves as a model of "lower-class expressions of the desire for a nonambiguous moral order."

Manifestations of social anxiety

But even so, wrestling in the 1950s was more than a struggle between good and evil. The basic allegory had four variations that clearly struck responsive chords with fans in postwar America. The first and most obvious of these was nationalism. Heels like Fritz Von Erich, who looked and acted as if he were a Nazi freshly mustered out of Hitler's army, or Ivan Koloff, who had a hammer and sickle tattooed on his biceps, were wrestlers U.S. audiences loved to hate and loved to see vanquished.

Villainy was usually linked to a second theme as well: hubris. Babyfaces were modest. They spoke softly and respected their opponents. Heels shouted and boasted, telling interviewers in explicit detail how they would dismember their foes. This kind of egotism, reverberating off Russian premier Nikita Krushchev's famous boast that he would bury us, needed to be punished.

A third theme was merit. Good wrestlers in those days were called "scientific," meaning they used the techniques of amateur wrestling—basically leverages and holds—in their combat. Bad wrestlers were "dirty," and would do anything to win. In the 1950s and '60s, the wars between scientific wrestlers and dirty ones were jihads for fairness in a dog-eat-dog world where fans worried about the new American mania for getting ahead, not to mention those underhanded Soviets again.

Finally, there was the theme of homophobia. Ever since Gorgeous George arrived on the scene in the late 1940s with his sequined orchid robes, his marcelled blond hair, and a valet who paraded around the ring spraying an atomizer filled with perfume, wrestling has had its preening pretty boys. Almost without exception, they have been heels, drawing boos for their mincing steps and grandiose vanity. In an entertainment that was rife with homoerotic overtones, hating the pretty boy was a graphic way of reaffirming one's own masculinity.

All of these themes were manifestations of social anxiety, but they were subsumed and soothed by one overriding principle: justice. "Wrestlers remain gods," Barthes writes, "because they are, for a few moments, the key which opens Nature, the pure gesture which separates Good from Evil. . . ." The anti-Americanism, the hubris, the dirtiness, and the gender-bending were all presented only to be defeated—so that one could rid this fictional world of what could not be exorcised from the real world. Like the movies of the 1950s, wrestling was a kind of wish fulfillment that made things right.

Revising wrestling's form

Today's wrestling evolved from this tradition and still borrows heavily from it, but the sport has also revised it. No single individual has been more responsible for that revision than Vince McMahon, who might be called professional wrestling's Steven Spielberg for the popularizing imagination he brought to the sport.

A third-generation wrestling promoter, the 53-year-old McMahon, who has the beefed-up, pompadoured look of a mob enforcer from a *Godfather* knockoff, bought a northeastern franchise from his father in 1982, then set about to drag wrestling from the Stone Age. His first innovation was tactical. Despite repeated attempts by various promoters over the years to consolidate and monopolize wrestling under one aegis, it had remained a regional affair with a plethora of local promotions or circuits, like McMahon's, each with its own wrestling stars, its own "world" champions, and its own local television contracts that usually relegated programs to Saturday afternoons or Sunday mornings. When McMahon bought Georgia Championship Wrestling in 1984, he began taking his World Wrestling Federation national, making himself not only wrestling's Spielberg but its Bill Gates as well. His temerity infuriated his competitors, but he created the only conditions under which wrestling could thrive: a national entertainment with national television exposure to sell pay-per-view events.

Like the movies of the 1950s, wrestling was a kind of wish fulfillment that made things right.

Having revolutionized the economic base of wrestling, McMahon also set out to change its form. He recognized the affinity between wrestling and rock 'n' roll—essentially understanding that the same flamboyance that energized rock concerts could also energize wrestling programs. The deafening din in the arena, the dramatic introductions of wrestlers on huge overhead screens while signature theme songs blared over the loudspeakers, the face-painting (inspired, he admitted, by the band Kiss), and the glam costumes were all endowments from rock, with the intended effect not only of drawing on the ethos of rock to modernize wrestling but of attracting rock's young audience.

Still, during its last boom in the mid-1980s, wrestling remained an old-fashioned allegory of justice dressed up in new garb. McMahon's biggest star, Hulk Hogan, who spearheaded the revival then, was a bleached-blond babyface whose job was to smote the heels just as the heroes of yore had done. Little Hulksters loved him, and he parlayed his popularity into a cottage industry: Hogan toys, Hogan movies, big Hogan pay-per-views. Even now, by one report, he earns $5 million a year.

By shoving wrestling back on the national scene, Hogan also gained McMahon a rival. As McMahon has told it, Ted Turner tried to buy WWF in the mid-1980s, when Turner's TBS network was garnering high ratings with McMahon's product. After McMahon rejected the bid, Turner began buying up a network of southern wrestling federations and redubbed the new entity World Championship Wrestling. WCW debuted on TBS in 1991. Two years later, Turner began poaching McMahon's talent, signing the stars Randy "Macho Man" Savage, Ric Flair, Kevin Nash, and Hulk Hogan himself.

With its bottomless pockets, WCW now had the upper hand, and it gained an even greater advantage in 1993, when McMahon was indicted on federal charges of distributing anabolic steroids to his wrestlers between 1985 and '91. For 83 straight weeks, WCW bested WWF in the ratings. To add insult to injury, Hogan himself testified at the trial, admitting that he had used steroids. With its biggest hero sullied and its promotion in turmoil, wrestling ratings fell, and attendance plummeted to half what it had been in 1991.

In the vast, ongoing power struggle that forms wrestling's master plot, wrestlers are constantly changing allegiances to fulfill their personal agendas.

But predictions of Vince McMahon's demise turned out to be just as premature as the pronouncements of doom that wrestling announcers routinely issue when a wrestler lies unconscious on the mat, only to rouse himself suddenly and miraculously get a pin. When McMahon was acquitted of all charges in July 1994, he seemed to have been revivified and sought to revive his empire as well. Having already borrowed successfully from rock, he began lifting from anything and everything in popular culture, from *Star Wars* to *Jerry Springer* to religious revivalists to adult porno movies, and grafting it onto wrestling, making WWF a new, capacious, voracious entertainment machine—a postmodernist mélange. If it was out there, wrestling had learned to assimilate it. "The WWF is a soap, it's an action adventure, it's a live-action cartoon, and it's part talk show," McMahon told *Entertainment Weekly*.

The larger framework for these new appropriations, and by far the most important of them, was what McMahon called the story line, meaning that wrestling was elaborating its narratives into sagas that continued from week to week just as the stories on conventional television shows did. In fact, the actual wrestling diminished, as longer, more convoluted plots that took wrestlers into their dressing rooms, the boiler room, the parking lot, and even down city streets were introduced. According to an analysis conducted at Indiana University between January 12, 1998, and February 1, 1999, for the television program *Inside Edition,* there was now so much storytelling on *Raw* that only 36 minutes of the two-hour broadcast featured wrestling matches.

The emergence of wrestling nation-states

One doesn't need a content analysis, however, to see that this is definitely not your father's wrestling. The first difference a newcomer notices is that wrestlers are no longer individual agents in *mano a mano* combat. Almost all of them are members of one faction or another—the wrestling equivalent of nation-states that are so numerous and complex, often with factions within factions, they would confound even a Balkans expert. WWF has the Ministry of Darkness and the Corporation, which, until his son deposed him, was headed by a character named Mr. McMahon, played with gusto, in a Pirandellian touch [after Italian author Luigi Pirandello], by Vince himself, who obviously does head the Corporation. When these two merged into the Corporate Ministry, another group of wrestlers, including Ken Shamrock, Mankind, and the Big Show, formed the Union to counter the new force. Meanwhile, the Ministry was itself spinning off another faction called the Brood, while a cluster of younger wrestlers, including X-Pac, Mr. Ass, and the Road Dogg, formed D-Generation X, with the slogan "Suck it!" Stone Cold Steve Austin, currently the most popular wrestler in the WWF, remains unaffiliated. He is his own man, hating all and being hated in turn by his fellow wrestlers.

Not to be outdone, WCW has its own corporate villain, former wrestling announcer turned executive Eric Bischoff, who, like McMahon, is the head of the outfit in real life. To defy the corporate powers, another group of wrestlers, including Hogan, formed the New World Order, which was itself subdivided into factions called the Wolfpac, the Black and White, and the Red. Challenging the NWO is the Four Horsemen, headed by the 50-year-old 13-time world wrestling champion Ric Flair, bitter enemy of Bischoff after Bischoff switched sides and engineered an NWO takeover of WCW. Standing alone outside all of them, like Austin in the WWF, is WCW's biggest star, Goldberg, a snarling destruction machine whose only loss came when Wolfpac member Scott Hall disguised himself as a security guard and stun-gunned Goldberg during a championship match.

Everywhere one looks in wrestling, someone is crossing the line, challenging the authorities, acting outrageously, disregarding taste and moral tradition.

In the vast, ongoing power struggle that forms wrestling's master plot, wrestlers are constantly changing allegiances to fulfill their personal agendas. Shane McMahon, claiming that his father always favored his sister Stephanie, got revenge by calling Vince into the ring and seizing the WWF in a putsch. "You want power?" the elder McMahon snarled. "You have to earn it with respect." To which Shane riposted, "Respect this," and slapped his father—"the slap heard round the world," as the announcers called it. That set in motion a series of confrontations between McMahon *père* [father] and *fils* [son], with Vince punching his son during a melee and Shane kicking his father after the Undertaker had whacked Vince senseless with a chair.

Meanwhile, in the WCW, Bischoff had humiliated Flair by slapping his son and kissing his wife. Flair, whose trademark is losing control, stripping down to his boxers and howling "Wooooo!" challenged Bischoff to a match for control of the entire WCW, which Flair won. Bischoff was now relegated to assisting the truck driver who carted the ring. But using the temptation of a mysterious blond siren, Flair's enemies convinced his son to sign commitment papers remanding the loopy Flair to an insane asylum.

As if this weren't enough, the Godfather, whose slogan is "Pimpin' ain't easy," fought Jeff Jarrett for the right to have Jarrett's well-endowed, skimpily clad girlfriend, Debra, join the Godfather's "Ho train"; Val Venis, ostensibly a onetime porn movie star, was locked in a dispute with the androgynous Goldust, who claims Venis impregnated his wife; Mankind, a paunchy introvert who wrestles in a boiler room, wears a leather mask and beats his opponents by sticking a dirty sock named Mr. Socko in their mouths, is being harassed by the Ministry; and Stone Cold Steve Austin continues his battle with the corporate powers who want to dethrone him, at one point driving a Big Wheel truck through the stadium barricades when McMahon had a security guard turn his four-by-four away, saying the parking lot was reserved for limousines.

It is utter silliness, this narrative phantasmagoria, but it also touches on the anxieties of viewers, just as the older, simpler narratives of the 1950s touched on the anxieties of their viewers. Here is infidelity, sexual desire, sibling rivalry, betrayal, mental illness, generational conflict, ageism for the sizable cohort of seniors in the audience (Flair is constantly being taunted by Bischoff for his age and being teased that he might suffer a heart attack), and, last but by no means least, the antagonism of the employee against the employer, of the individual against the system. About the only issue that isn't addressed is race, perhaps because it is so sensitive it might threaten the comforting basis of the entertainment, which is to take these topics and safely displace them from real life into the ring.

Crossing moral lines

What really differentiates these new narratives from the old ones, though, is not just their obvious variety, complexity and increased sexual explicitness, but something more substantive: their lack of moral clarity. In the past, a heel could turn babyface and babyface could turn heel, but one always understood the moral fault lines that divided one character from the other. That morality is much less intelligible now. The Rock is a braggart who favors expensive cars and jewelry, who calls the fans "trailer park trash" and who once groused of the homeless that as long as he had his "palatial palace down in South Beach in Miami, Florida, he really couldn't give a damn whether or not they live in a Frigidaire box or a Kenmore box," yet the Rock is called the People's Champion. Hogan has grown dark beard stubble, changed his name to Hollywood to signify that he has "gone Hollywood," and fights dirty. But if he is the bad guy, there is no good guy on the other side, save Goldberg and another wrestler named Sting. Ken Shamrock, the "world's most dangerous man," is likable and decent, but he has defended McMahon who, as boss, is without question the most detested man in wrestling. And so it goes. Because no one is fighting for a transcendent cause but only for power or vindication or vengeance or money, no one is on the side of right.

> *By creating a perception of disreputability around wrestling, [McMahon] has helped make it not only an expression of transgression but a way for millions of fans to exercise their own transgressive impulses.*

For Barthes, as for most fans of the old wrestling, right was a necessary ingredient for the allegory. Without it, there could be no justice. But the new wrestling is not about justice. Its overriding and inescapable theme—whether the story has the NWO trying to take control of WCW or Debra showing off her "puppies" or Steve Austin crushing open beer cans after a victory and guzzling the brew—is transgression. Everywhere one looks in wrestling, someone is crossing the line, challenging the authorities, acting outrageously, disregarding taste and moral tradition. Good and bad have no place in this corrupt universe. Only outlawry does. All of which is neatly summarized in Austin's trademark gesture: flipping the finger to the world.

The liberation of wrestling

"Is it fake?" That had always been the ultimate question when it came to professional wrestling—the one that kept it poised between sport and show, reality and fantasy. Promoters had always assumed that, while the fans obviously enjoyed the machinations that enlivened the sport and provided its themes, these same fans didn't want their wrestling to be demystified. So they insisted that the sport was real, even though any intelligent fan knew the jig and maintained a silent conspiracy with the lords of wrestling.

But even as half a sport, wrestling invited government regulation—something that no one in the game desired. As a result, Vince McMahon began to suggest publicly what everyone already knew: Wrestling was fixed but it wasn't exactly faked, since wrestlers did actually perform those stunts in the ring and could be injured or worse. In May 1999, Owen "the Blue Blazer" Hart was killed when he fell some 60 feet as he was being lowered into the ring by a cable. As Bischoff put it, "We are not fake sports. We are a real entertainment."

The revelation stirred surprisingly little comment or interest. Mainly, it spurred New Jersey governor Christie Todd Whitman to call for a bill that would recognize wrestling as an entertainment, the passage of which deregulated wrestling as an industry and exempted it from a special state media tax. But the broad acceptance of wrestling as a show did have a radicalizing effect on the form. No longer bound by any pretense of reality, wrestling was liberated to do anything it wanted to do, which led to the new outrageousness of leather-masked men wrestling in boiler rooms, scantily clad female managers baring their breasts to distract their wrestler's opponent, and rednecks dumping cement into their boss's Corvette, as Austin did to McMahon.

Perhaps even more important, the acceptance of wrestling as entertainment has fundamentally changed the audience's relationship to the show. With the conspiracy of silence broken, fans too were liberated to treat the whole thing as a giant goof—not an athletic competition but a hilarious parody of the greed, aggression, overcommercialization, and criminality that was overwhelming legitimate sports. Indeed, the enthusiasts played an active role in the parody. If wrestling was an entertainment pretending to be a sport, they were an audience pretending to be fans—gleefully shouting "Suck it!" with D-Generation X, waving giant foam middle fingers, or chanting "Goldberg" with full appreciation of the stereotype-smashing comedy that was inherent in the situation of a Jewish wrestler's being the most-feared man in the game.

With the whole spectacle a kind of huge in-joke, true fans pride themselves on "getting it," which is a familiar term among WWF enthusiasts who occasionally hold up signs announcing I GET IT! as if they were religious zealots at an evangelical convocation declaring their faith. To "get it" means you understand that none of it is to be taken seriously, that it is really another put-on, like Howard Stern and Jerry Springer—an awareness that turns wrestling into a litmus test of cultural intelligence to distinguish those who are cool enough to recognize the joke from those who aren't.

To those who don't get it, the knock on wrestling is that it is a low-brow entertainment for a lowbrow audience. Even as its marketers talk up advertisers about younger, more affluent fans, the new wrestling doesn't dispute that characterization but, rather, actively promotes it. "Please say that we are out of control, please say that," McMahon told *Broadcasting & Cable* magazine. "The more our competitors talk about how aggressive we are, the bad language and all that, the better off we'll be."

Thumbing a nose at polite society

In a way, that may be McMahon's greatest ploy. By creating a perception of disreputability around wrestling, he has helped make it not only an expression of transgression but a way for millions of fans to exercise their own transgressive impulses. Told by critics that wrestling is idiotic or disgusting, they can, by the simple act of watching it, play Steve Austin to genteel society's Mr. McMahon, thus placing themselves in the long tradition of American cultural contrarianism. The louder, the dumber, the crazier, the better. One sign held proudly aloft at a recent event said it all: TRAILER PARK TRASH.

Wrestling is largely being watched by young, lower-middle-class men—the very group that is likely to feel disempowered.

This is what wrestling devotees mean when they brag that wrestling has "attitude"—a word that is emblazoned on WWF T-shirts, scrawled on placards at arenas, and impregnated into the entertainment itself. Attitude is the way Austin swaggers around the ring with his impassive scowl, the way Diamond Dallas Page thrusts his championship belt at fans, and the way McMahon sneers at his critics, but it is also the way fans luxuriate in the faux amoralism of their faux sport, and it is what drives the anti-wrestling moralists crazy. If "getting it" helps explain why being a wrestling fan is considered cool now, "attitude"—shouting "Asshole" at McMahon as he enters the ring or screaming epithets at Bischoff—helps explain why fans find wrestling so cathartic. It's that finger to the world again, only this time they're the ones who are flashing it.

Still, understanding the exhilaration that now suffuses wrestling is hard without knowing just who these fans really are. A Nielsen survey of WCW television viewers covering the first half of 1998 found that 51 percent of them were males 18 years and older, and 12 percent were teens 12 to 17 years old; 25 percent were females 18 and over; 38 percent were high school graduates; 23 percent had one to three years of college; 11 percent were college graduates; 43 percent were blue-collar; 26 percent were students and retirees; 31 percent were white-collar; 26 percent earned $50,000 or more in income; 43 percent earned $20,000 to $50,000; and 31 percent earned $20,000 or less. WWF demographics were virtually identical: a little less than 50 percent males 18 and over; a little less than 25 percent females 18 and over. What is more significant for advertisers, however, is that the most popular wrestling program, *Raw Is War,* on the USA cable network, has been attracting more males aged 18 to 34, the prime demographic for disposable income, than any other program on television—cable or broadcast. In short, wrestling is largely being watched by young, lower-middle-class men—the very group that is likely to feel disempowered.

The central dispute now between WWF and WCW is how to enlarge that fan base and the advertising revenue that comes with it. WWF clearly believes that the more downscale the entertainment, the more young males there will be who want to use it to thumb their noses at polite society, which is why WWF programs regularly feature simulated sex (128 times, according to the yearlong Indiana University study), crotch-grabbing (1,658 times), flipping the finger (157 times), and prostitutes (20 times). So far, it is working. After regularly being beaten by WCW's *Nitro, Raw* outdrew it by an average of 34.7 percent of viewers between September 1998 and May 1999, and by 56.4 percent between February and May—the very period during which critics were complaining about WWF's raunch.

WCW, on the other hand, believes that by domesticating the transgressive elements such as overt sex and foul language, it can go mainstream and attract an even larger, more upscale audience, one that includes families. And Bischoff fretted to one interviewer that after years of wrestling "being thought of as a low-rent form of entertainment, [McMahon] is further stigmatizing our genre as not a good place [for advertisers] to be."

The direction of wrestling may very well be determined by which strategy prevails—whether wrestling can continue to slide downscale without marginalizing itself or whether it can go upscale without destroying the populism that is its very lifeblood. At this moment, however, as it straddles the bottom and the middle, wrestling may be both America's most amazing pop culture pastiche and its most powerful form of populist therapy. In wrestling, grievances are redressed, anger is vented, the imbalance of power is equalized, outsiders become insiders, and the culturally dispossessed are enfranchised as the only people who really get it. That's why so many fans love it. In wrestling, at long last, ordinary guys can tell the whole world to go to hell.

Organizations and Websites

The editors have compiled the following list of organizations and websites concerned with the issues presented in this book. Descriptions are derived from materials provided by the organizations. All have publications or information available for interested readers. The list was compiled on the date of publication of the present volume; the information presented here may change. Be aware that many organizations take several weeks or longer to respond to inquiries, so allow as much time as possible.

Center for Parent/Youth Understanding (CPYU)
PO Box 414, Elizabethtown, PA 17022
(717) 361-8429 • fax: (717) 361-8964
e-mail: cpyuinfo@aol.com • website: www.cpyu.org

CPYU is a nonprofit organization whose goal is to build strong families by providing a bridge across the cultural-generational gap between parents and teenagers. The center provides information, resources, and analysis on today's youth culture for those charged with helping teenagers. CPYU publishes analysis of youth culture in its *In the Hotlight* pamphlets and a quarterly newsletter *youthculture@today*. On its website the center provides access to many of its resources, including the book *Understanding Today's Youth Culture* and newsletter articles such as "My Week in Professional Wrestling" and "What You Need to Know About Television Violence."

Media Research Center (MRC)
325 S. Patrick St., Alexandria, VA 22314
(703) 683-9733 • fax: (703) 683-9736
e-mail: mrc@mediaresearch.org • website: www.mediaresearch.org

MRC's goal is to bring political balance to the nation's news media and responsibility to the entertainment media. The center tapes news and entertainment shows to identify liberal bias, and MRC spokesmen appear on network television programs and provide editors and producers with information on conservative positions to balance liberal views. MRC President Brent Bozell writes a weekly newspaper column on media and entertainment issues, including "Veni, Vidi, Vince: McMahon's Manifesto," which can be found on the MRC website. Also on its website, MRC provides access to *CyberAlert*, a publication that reveals what MRC believes to be the latest examples of liberal media bias and irresponsibility in the entertainment media.

National Institute on Media and the Family
606 24th Ave. South, Suite 606, Minneapolis, MN 55454
(888) 672-5437 • fax: (612) 672-4113
e-mail: information@mediafamily.org • website: www.mediafamily.org

The National Institute on Media and the Family is a nonprofit, nonpartisan organization created as a national resource for research, education, and information about the impact of media on children and families. Its mission is to maximize the benefits and minimize the harm of media on children and families through research and education. The institute provides parents and other adults with information about media products and their likely impact on children. It does not advocate censorship of any kind, but is committed to partnering with parents and other caregivers, organizations, and corporations in using the power of the free market to create a healthier media diet for families and therefore create healthier, less violent communities. On its website the institute publishes fact sheets, including "TV, Professional Wrestling, and Children."

Parents Television Council (PTC)
707 Wilshire Blvd. #1950, Los Angeles, CA 90017
(213) 629-9255
website: www.parentstv.org

Established in 1995, the PTC is a nonprofit organization whose goal is to persuade the entertainment industry to provide positive, family-oriented television programming. The council believes that the gratuitous sex, foul language, and violence on TV have a negative effect on children. It aims to motivate the public to voice their support for family-friendly programming to network executives, advertisers, public policy leaders, and the creative community in Hollywood. The PTC publishes the *Family Guide,* which profiles programming on the major television networks, provides information on inappropriate subject matter for children, and identifies shows which promote family-friendly themes. The Council also publishes the monthly *PTC Insider* and a yearly *Top 10 List* that reveals the latest family-friendly TV shows. On its website the PTC provides access to its publications as well as special reports, news alerts, and commentary, including "Taking on WWF *Smackdown!*"

Rock Out Censorship (ROC)
PO Box 147, Jewett, OH 43986
(740) 946-2011
e-mail: roc@theroc.org • website: www.theroc.org

The primary goal of ROC has been to oppose censorship in the music industry, but ROC also opposes the entire spectrum of censorship activity. The organization was originally formed in 1989 to oppose the Parent's Music Resource Center (PMRC), which supported the placement of warning labels on record albums. ROC maintains that these stickers do very little to warn parents, but instead open the door to more restrictive forms of censorship. To inform the public of censorship and other constitutional issues, the ROC sets up anticensorship booths at major concert events across the country and publishes a twenty-four-page newspaper, *THE ROC.* On its website ROC provides news concerning censorship in entertainment and the arts, on the Internet, and at schools and universities. The website also provides access to current issues as well as archives of *THE ROC* newspaper.

World Wrestling Federation Entertainment, Inc. (WWFE)
1241 East Main St., Stamford, CT 06902
(203) 352-8600
website: www.wwf.com

WWFE is a media and entertainment company engaged in the development, production, and marketing of television, pay-per-view programming, and live wrestling events and the licensing and sale of consumer products. WWFE publishes several magazines, including *WWF, RAW,* and *EXTREME,* and autobiographies of WWF superstars, including *The Rock Says.* On its website WWFE provides streaming video of live events, publishes pro wrestling news, commentary, and excerpts from current issues of its magazines, and supports links to its website, WWF Parents.

Websites

Pro Wrestling Torch
www.pwtorch.com

The Pro Wrestling Torch is an online journal of wrestling news and opinion that serves as a supplement to the in-depth coverage found in the *Pro Wrestling Torch Weekly*, a twelve-page print newsletter. The website provides access to *Pro Wrestling Torch Weekly* archives, a wrestling glossary, and interviews with pro wrestling stars.

World Wrestling Federation (WWF) Parents
www.wwfparents.com

WWF Parents is a website maintained by World Wrestling Federation Entertainment, Inc. (WWFE). It encourages parents to help their children select suitable entertainment and to understand the differences between fantasy and real life. WWF Parents provides resources to help parents talk to their children about the issues they face, including "Parents to Parents," where participants share positive uses of WWF programming and "WWFE Advice," which includes WWFE's stance opposing backyard wrestling and explains that WWF performers are trained athletes. The website also promotes the WWF *Get REAL* program, which encourages children to pursue respect, education, achievement, and leadership.

Wrestling Fans Against Censorship (WFAC)
http://wfac.cjb.net

WFAC was founded to form a united front against the Parents Television Council (PTC), which urges advertisers to remove their sponsorship of *WWF Smackdown!* and other WWF programming. WFAC bands together thousands of pro wrestling fans and over two hundred websites to oppose the PTC. On its website, the WFAC provides links to sponsors who both support and oppose the WWF, encouraging fans to voice their support of WWF sponsors and their dissatisfaction to those sponsors who have withdrawn support from the WWF. The website maintains news and updates of PTC censorship efforts and releases its own research to counter what the WFAC believes to be misinformation distributed by the PTC.

Wrestling Observer
www.liveaudlpwrestling.com/wo

The Wrestling Observer is an online journal of wrestling news and commentary. On its website, the Wrestling Observer features wrestling headlines, interviews, and excerpts from its print newsletter, the *Wrestling Observer Newsletter*. The website also provides access to *Live Audio Wrestling*, also known as *LAW* radio, an online wrestling talk radio program.

Bibliography

Books

Jeff Archer

Theater in a Squared Circle. Lafayette, CO: White-Boucke, 1998.

Michael R. Ball

Professional Wrestling as Ritual Drama in American Popular Culture. Lewiston, NY: Mellen, Edwin, 1990.

Keith Elliot and Elliot Greenberg

The History of Pro Wrestling: From Carnivals to Cable TV, Minneapolis: Lerner Publishing Group, 2001.

Mick Foley

Foley Is Good: And the Real Word Is Faker than Wrestling. New York: Regan Books, 2001.

Scott Keith and John Craddock

The Buzz on Professional Wrestling. New York: Lebhar-Friedman Books, 2001.

Sharon Mazer

Professional Wrestling: Sport and Spectacle. Jackson: University Press of Mississippi, 1998.

Gerald W. Morton and George M. O'Brien

Wrestling to Rasslin: Ancient Sport to American Spectacle. Bowling Green, OH: Bowling Green State University Popular Press, 1985.

Irwin Wilbur Stanton

Trouble in Paradise: Behind the Scenes of Amateur and Professional Wrestling—Behind the Cameras of Network Television. New York: Vantage Press, 1991.

Periodicals

Katy Abel

"Kids Get Slammed by Pro Wrestling," *familyeducation.com*, April 13, 2000. http://familyeducation.com/article/0,1120,1-9550,00.html.

L. Brent Bozell III

"Veni, Vidi, Vince: McMahon's Manifesto," *Media Research Center*, October 17, 2000. www.mediaresearch.org/columns/entcol/col20001017.html.

Ron Buck

"True Confessions: Inside the Mind of a 'Rasslin Fan," *ESPN.com: Outside the Lines*, April 2, 1999. http://espn.go.com/otl/wrestling/day_1part1.html.

John W. Campbell

"ProfessionalWrestling: Why the Bad Guy Wins," *Journal of American Culture*, Summer 1996. Available from Pat Browne, Popular Press, Bowling Green University, Bowling Green, OH 43403.

Connie Chung and Deborah Roberts, narrators

"Backyard Wrestling," *20/20*, ABC, August 25, 1999. http://abcnews.go.com/onair/2020/transcripts/2020_990825_wrestling_trans.html.

Economist

"Professional Wrestling: Kiss My Ass," August 28, 1999.

Mike Flaherty and Lynette Rice	"Big Smack: WWF SMACKDOWN!'S Powerful Ratings Have UPN Saying, WHAM! BAM! Thank You, Vince McMahon," *EW.com*, November 1, 1999.
Jonah Goldberg	"Body Slam: The Stupid and Demagogic Rhetoric of Jesse Ventura," *National Review*, October 9, 2000.
Lewis Gorssberger	"Rassle Dazzle," *MediaWeek*, December 14, 1998. Available from MediaWeek Reprint Services, (651) 582-3800.
Zondra Hughes	"The Rock Talks About Race, Wrestling, and Women," *Ebony*, July 2001.
Louis Jacobson	"Getting Beyond Charisma," *National Journal*, October 28, 2000. (Profiles Minnesota governor Jesse Ventura.) Available from National Journal Group Inc., 1501 M St. NW, Suite 300, Washington, DC 20005. http://nationaljournal.com/help/reprints.htm#back.
Eric E. Jenkins	"What More Could Wrestling Have Done?" *WrestlingLife.com*, February 8, 2001. http://wrestloholic.hypermart.net/mag/headlines/337.html.
John W. Kennedy	"Redeemed Bad Boys of the WWF," *Christianity Today*, May 22, 2000.
Steve Klein	"Grappling with Wrestling Content," *Online Journalism Review*, June 7, 1999. http://ojr.usc.edu/content/story.cfm?request+134.
Jim Klobuchar	"Letting Jesse Be Jesse," *Christian Science Monitor*, March 1, 2001.
John Leland	"Stone Cold Crazy!" *Newsweek*, November 23, 1998.
John Leland	"Why America's Hooked on Wrestling," *Newsweek*, February 7, 2000.
Bob Levin	"A Groin Grab for Ratings," *Maclean's*, July 26, 1999.
Larry McShane	"Wrestling's Ultimate Match: Ted vs. Vince, Winner-Take-All," *Reporter-news.com*, June 27, 1999. www.reporternews.com/1999/biz/wrestle0627.html.
Devin D. O'Leary	"Does TV Wrestling Need a Bodyslam?" *Alibi Film*, June 24–30, 1999. www.weeklywire.com/alibi/1999-06-24/idiotbox.html.
Parents Television Council	"What a Difference a Decade Makes," April 25, 2000. www.parentstv.org/publications/reports/Decadestudy/decadecover.html.
Ray Ratto	"Take Vince McMahon Seriously—Honest," *ESPN.com*, February 4, 2001. http://espn.go.com/columns/ratto_ray/335256.html.
Rick Reilly	"Kids Are Trying This at Home," *Sports Illustrated*, February 12, 2001.
Kevin Udahl	"Last Count for the Blue Blazer," *Alberta Report*, June 7, 1999. Available from United Western Communications Ltd., 17327 106A Ave., Edmonton, Alberta T5S 1M7. http://albertareport.com/volume26/990607/story3.html.

Index